The Freshfields Guide to Arbitration and ADR
Clauses in International Contracts

The Freshfields Guide to Arbitration and ADR

Clauses in International Contracts

Jan Paulsson

Nigel Rawding

Lucy Reed

Eric Schwartz

2nd revised edition

1999

KLUWER LAW INTERNATIONAL

THE HAGUE – LONDON – BOSTON

Published by:
Kluwer Law International
P.O. Box 85889, 2508 CN The Hague, The Netherlands

Sold and Distributed in North, Central and South America by:
Kluwer Law International
657 Massachusetts Avenue, Cambridge, MA 02139, USA

Sold and Distributed in all other countries by:
Kluwer Law International
Distribution Centre, P.O. Box 322, 3300 AH Dordrecht, The Netherlands

Library of Congress Cataloging-in-Publication Data is available from the Library of Congress

Printed on acid-free paper
Cover design: Alfred Birnie bNO

ISBN 90 411 1226 X

Kluwer Law International incorporates the publishing programmes
of Graham & Trotman Ltd, Kluwer Law and Taxation Publishers
and Martinus Nijhoff Publishers

3-0301-1500 ts

About the authors

The first edition of this Guide was the creation of Martin Hunter, Jan Paulsson, Nigel Rawding and Alan Redfern at a time when they were all partners in Freshfields and members of the firm's international arbitration group. Since retiring from the firm, Martin Hunter and Alan Redfern continue to feature prominently in the practice of international dispute resolution, sitting frequently as arbitrators as well as writing and speaking on the subject.

Jan Paulsson and Nigel Rawding continue as partners in the firm and members of the international arbitration group. They have been joined in recent times by other distinguished practitioners in the field, in Eric Schwartz (based in Paris), formerly the Secretary General of the ICC's International Court of Arbitration, and Lucy Reed (based in New York), former US Agent at the Iran-US Claims Tribunal, as members of the group and co-authors of this second edition.

Table of Contents

TABLE OF CONTENTS

TABLE OF CONTENTS

TABLE OF CONTENTS

Preface to the first edition

The dispute resolution clause is usually found near the end of a contract, alongside such innocuous items as addresses for serving notices. It may ultimately prove to be the most important provision of all. Rights and obligations carefully defined elsewhere in the contract are only as reliable as the courts or tribunals called upon to give effect to them.

Yet with astonishing regularity international contracts contain defective dispute resolution clauses. Even lengthy and complex agreements, drafted by negotiators whose understanding of everything else is highly sophisticated, often reflect ignorance of the mechanisms of international dispute resolution. Hence this concise Guide, designed for contract negotiators.

Other negotiating options are available in contemporary practice to those who are dissatisfied with traditional adjudicatory mechanisms. These options have in recent years been described by the acronym ADR ("alternative dispute resolution"). The Guide addresses some of the most important features of ADR and includes some suggested model ADR clauses.

Naturally, the Guide cannot be relied upon as a substitute for specialist professional advice as to the appropriate method of dispute resolution in the particular circumstances of any individual transaction. The international scene is constantly changing. Today's preferred solution will not necessarily be tomorrow's. However, the *types* of pitfalls tend to remain the same and one of the aims of this Guide is to help steer the reader away from them.

The focus of this Guide is Chapter 7 – "Drafting the arbitration clause". For the harried practitioner, it may be the first section to be consulted at the eleventh hour of a negotiation, together with the model clauses set out in Appendix 1. But with arbitration clauses, as with a balance sheet, to achieve a proper understanding requires more than looking at the bottom line.

Preface to the second edition

In introducing this second edition of the Guide it is tempting to say something which is at least new, even if not profound. There have been significant developments in the law and practice of international arbitration since the publication of the first edition in 1993, notably in the promulgation of new arbitration laws and new or revised international arbitration rules. Yet the considerations which prompted us to prepare the Guide in the first place have not changed. It is still true that relatively little attention is paid to the dispute resolution clause in otherwise lengthy, complex and heavily negotiated agreements. The *raison d'être* for the Guide therefore remains the same, as does the advice – albeit updated in order to take account of recent developments – that follows.

1

Choosing the method

In broad terms, contract disputes may be resolved by:
- direct negotiation,
- one of the many forms of alternative dispute resolution,
- arbitration, or
- litigation before national courts.

In contrast to *domestic* contracts (where all concerned expect the local national courts to have jurisdiction, even in the absence of a contractual provision to that effect), parties to *international* contracts need to agree on what will happen if a dispute cannot be resolved by negotiation. This is best done at the time of negotiating the contract.

National courts

Parties occasionally designate a national court as the forum for resolving disputes. But in most international transactions (with the possible exception of those concerned solely with lending money or other standard form transactions), it is unlikely that the same national court will be accepted by both sides. This is because most parties are unwilling to permit disputes to be determined in the other side's home territory. Nor are the courts of a third, neutral, country likely to be appropriate, for several reasons.

First, it may be unwise to entrust a dispute governed by a different, or "foreign", system of law to national judges whose qualifications and training are deeply rooted in their own legal systems.

Secondly, the contract, and all correspondence and documents relating to the dispute, may have to be translated into the working language of the judge of the national court. Furthermore, the oral proceedings will necessarily have to be in the judge's own language, which means that those most closely connected with the transaction may not understand what is being said – or may not be able to make themselves understood – and that advocates unfamiliar with the parties and the transaction may have to be retained to play the lead role.

Thirdly, it is not always certain that the courts of a country having no connection with either the parties or the subject matter of the dispute will allow their judicial resources (generally paid for by that country's taxpayers) to be used for resolving disputes between "foreign" parties. The jurisdiction of a chosen national court may also be open to attack by one of the parties on grounds of *forum non conveniens*, notwithstanding the agreement to refer the dispute to those courts.

Fourthly, with some exceptions (e.g. cases within the European Union) the network of treaties for the recognition of national court judgments is incomplete. By contrast, arbitration awards are more readily enforceable across national frontiers than judgments of national courts, particularly when the losing party has refused or failed to appear in the proceedings.

Fifthly, court actions are open to public scrutiny.

Arbitration

By contrast with litigation before national courts, arbitration is a private, consensual process (in the sense that it is derived from the parties' agreement to refer disputes to arbitration). It is nevertheless intended to result in a binding, enforceable award.

CHOOSING THE METHOD

Although circumscribed by the parties' agreement, most standard form arbitration clauses cover claims for breach of contract, specific performance, misrepresentation and other claims "arising out of or in connection with" the contract. Examples of such standard clauses are included in Appendix 1.

The main *advantages* of international arbitration over litigation before national courts may be summarised as follows:

Neutrality

The arbitral tribunal and the procedure for the arbitration can be chosen so as to have a non-national character, acceptable to parties, their representatives and arbitrators from different legal and cultural backgrounds.

Confidentiality

Arbitration is a private process and the confidential nature of the dispute and the proceedings can generally be protected.

Procedural flexibility

The parties are free to choose the procedure which suits them best. They are not bound by national procedural rules.

Expert arbitrators

Arbitrators can be selected to fit the particular needs of the case, for example, where specific technical knowledge, qualifications or experience are required.

CHOOSING THE METHOD

Speed and cost

The flexibility of the arbitration procedure can lead to savings of both time and money. The time and cost involved will depend on the procedure adopted, the degree of co-operation between the parties, the availability of the arbitrators, and the fees charged by them.

Finality of Awards

Appeals by either party or other recourse to national courts may be restricted or excluded by law or by agreement between the parties.

Enforcement of Awards

Foreign arbitration awards are enforceable in more than 120 countries which are parties to the 1958 New York Convention on the Recognition and Enforcement of Foreign Arbitral Awards: see Chapter 3 and Appendix 5.

There are, however, potential *disadvantages* in the use of arbitration as opposed to litigation, the significance of which will depend upon the circumstances of each case:

Limited powers of arbitrators

Arbitrators lack effective powers of compulsion. In certain cases it may be necessary for the parties to have recourse to the national courts, e.g. for injunctions or other forms of interim relief which carry effective sanctions and can bind third parties. (Many arbitration rules expressly provide that applications to the courts for such interim relief are not incompatible with the agreement to arbitrate.)

CHOOSING THE METHOD

Multi-party disputes

In general, an arbitral tribunal has no power to join third parties (i.e. persons who are not parties to the arbitration agreement) into arbitration proceedings against their will, nor to order the consolidation of two or more arbitrations without the consent of all parties, even where common questions of fact or law arise which affect all parties. Also, even where all parties agree to the consolidation of separate arbitration proceedings, practical difficulties can arise since workable procedures for multi-party arbitrations are rarely provided for in pre-existing arbitration rules.

Awards not binding on third parties

An arbitral award cannot generally bind a third party who has not participated in the proceedings, nor establish a binding legal precedent for future proceedings.

A compromise solution?

To some extent, there remains the perception that a major disadvantage of arbitration is that the arbitrator may try to reach a compromise decision and may be reluctant to find unequivocally in favour of one party or the other. In reality, however, the perception that arbitrators have a tendency to "split the baby" is unwarranted. Unless expressly authorised to do otherwise (for example to decide the dispute *ex aequo et bono*), the arbitrator can be expected to decide the case in accordance with the rights of the parties under the contract and the applicable law.

Institutional or *ad hoc* arbitration?

Arbitrations may be conducted under the auspices of one of a number of international arbitral institutions or may be handled *ad hoc*, using rules tailored to the specific requirements of the parties and the circumstances of the case.

Institutional arbitration

The best known, and most frequently called-upon, international arbitral institutions are the International Court of Arbitration of the International Chamber of Commerce (*ICC*) and the London Court of International Arbitration (*LCIA*). Both the ICC and the LCIA have adopted new arbitration rules, effective from 1 January 1998.

Other prominent institutions include the International Centre for Settlement of Investment Disputes (*ICSID*) for use in investment disputes between states or state agencies and nationals of other states; the American Arbitration Association (*AAA*) whose own international rules were revised with effect from 1 April 1997; the Stockholm Chamber of Commerce; and a variety of regional institutions.

There are also a growing number of institutions catering for disputes arising in a particular trade area or industry, such as the World Intellectual Property Organisation (*WIPO*) and multilateral treaty-based systems such as the Energy Charter Treaty and the North American Free Trade Agreement (*NAFTA*).

Ad hoc arbitration

Ad hoc arbitration may be approached in either of the following ways:

Specially devised rules

Parties and their advisers may develop their own rules to govern the arbitration procedure, taking account of the nature of the particular dispute. However, preparing tailor-made rules in this way can prove to be expensive and time-consuming, and can lead to costly mistakes if the contract drafters fail to anticipate problems.

Adoption of the UNCITRAL Arbitration Rules

These rules were adopted by the United Nations Commission on International Trade Law *(UNCITRAL)* in 1976 and have achieved wide international recognition. They are intended for use by parties who wish to avoid involving an arbitral institution but wish to have a set of generally accepted rules available to them. If the UNCITRAL Rules are adopted, an appointing authority should be chosen, for example to select arbitrators if parties fail to do so.

The selection of appropriate arbitration rules, including those published by the ICC, the LCIA and UNCITRAL, is addressed in Chapter 5: Choosing the Rules.

ADR

Although arbitration itself is an alternative to recourse to the courts, it should be distinguished from methods of dispute resolution conventionally designated as alternative dispute resolution or "ADR".

Arbitration is intended to lead to a binding determination of a dispute, enforceable if necessary through execution against the assets of the losing party. To prevent injustice, the courts may set aside or refuse to enforce awards when the arbitral tribunal has not complied with certain essential requirements of natural justice or due process – such as treating the parties with equality, and giving each of them an adequate opportunity to present its case.

By contrast, ADR (in the narrow sense, excluding arbitration) is not usually intended to result in a *binding* determination of rights and obligations. Accordingly, the courts will not intervene to protect related procedural rights. In ADR, the victim of an abuse of process may simply reject the outcome of an ADR procedure – or refuse to participate in it all.

ADR procedures may take many forms, from third-party assisted negotiation to "mini trials". The procedures may be more or less sophisticated and more or less formalised or structured. They may be described as facilitative or evaluative, interest-based or rights-based. They may take the form of contractual obligations to have personnel of a certain level participate in discussions at early stages of a dispute, or to seek an "early neutral evaluation" of the merits of each party's case, by an independent third party.

Contracts often provide for a "cooling off" period in which parties agree not to take any formal step (such as commencing an arbitration) for a given period in order to allow an opportunity for their dispute to be resolved by other means. The involvement of a perceptive, diplomatic and businesslike outsider may tilt the discussions toward accommodation rather than discord. Insofar as the result depends upon its acceptability to all parties concerned, it has in one sense been achieved through negotiation. Alternatively, the availability of even an informal, non-binding view from a respected third party may in practice decide one or more of the issues and lead to an overall resolution, even if one party is unhappy with the outcome.

As the acronym ADR includes the concept "alternative", it may induce the belief that an ADR clause is a *substitute* for a traditional forum clause. It most certainly is not. A century ago, Theodore Roosevelt gave the advice to speak softly but carry a big stick. There have been many instances since then of the use of diplomacy coupled with the threat of force.

CHOOSING THE METHOD

Speaking softly will often do the job if both parties proceed in good faith. That is what ADR is all about.

Nonetheless, the fact is that most parties wish ultimately to be able to rely upon their contractual rights. However willing they may be to pursue negotiations, they understandably have no intention of giving up the stick of a binding procedure if they feel that they are entitled to substantially more than the other party is willing to offer.

ADR does not usually provide a mechanism to obtain a binding result. If it did, it would no longer be ADR but arbitration. The more the ADR process is successful in reaching settlement, the fewer arbitrations there will be. But it is just as true that greater use of ADR clauses should have no effect on the frequency of the inclusion of arbitration clauses in international contracts. A disputes clause without an ADR clause may perhaps not be ideal, but at least it can be made to work irrespective of the objections of a recalcitrant party. An ADR clause without a traditional binding disputes clause, at least in the international context, is a recipe for disaster.

In the following chapters, we set out the basic choices which the contract negotiator must make in deciding upon an effective mechanism for dealing with future disputes, starting with the applicable law, then the place of arbitration, the language of the arbitration, the rules to be applied and the selection of arbitrators. This is followed by a checklist for drafting arbitration clauses and a chapter devoted to intermediate dispute resolution and ADR.

2

Choosing the applicable law

Contract negotiators need to consider at an early stage what
law or rules of law will govern the parties' substantive rights
and obligations under the contract. But that is not the end of
the matter. At least five different systems of law may become
relevant during the course of an international arbitration. As
well as the law applicable to the substance of the dispute, it is
necessary to consider:

- the law that determines the capacity of the parties,
- the law that determines the validity of the arbitration
  agreement,
- the law governing the arbitration itself (in particular the
  procedure),
- if there is a conflict of applicable substantive laws, the law
  under which that conflict is to be resolved.

It may also be necessary to have regard to the law of the
likely place of *enforcement* of the award in order to anticipate
problems that may subsequently arise at the enforcement
stage.

   In general, the parties cannot make a choice of the law
applicable to capacity, except (for instance) by incorporating a
company in a particular country. The parties generally need
not make an express choice in relation either to the law governing the validity of the arbitration agreement or the law
governing the procedure of the arbitration itself. This will
usually follow naturally from the circumstances; the proper
law of the arbitration agreement is generally that of the contract of which it is a part, and the law governing the conduct

of the arbitration is generally that of the place or seat of arbitration. Parties wishing to make explicit exceptions in either respect should take specialist advice before doing so.

Some negotiators have the impression that by opting for arbitration in country X they have chosen the law of that country to govern the merits of any dispute. This is a mistake, attributable perhaps to the traditional notion in some legal systems that submission to a *national court* involves the implied acceptance of its substantive law. This is an alien concept in international arbitration, where the law of the place of arbitration has a strong claim to govern the conduct of the proceedings; a claim to influence (but no more) the resolution of conflict of laws; and no claim at all to govern substantive issues.

In practice, parties sometimes fail to choose any substantive law, thus leaving it to be determined by the arbitral tribunal. This may lead to the application of a system of law which is inappropriate to the language of the contract or to the intention of the parties. The parties should therefore try to resolve the question of the substantive (or proper) law at the time of negotiating the contract.

The many important consequences of the choice of applicable law are beyond the scope of this Guide. But since we are concerned with the ways of putting in place a reliable arbitral mechanism, the reader is invited to reflect on the likelihood that − in the absence of a provision to the contrary − the proper law of the contract will also be deemed to determine the validity, scope and effect of the arbitration clause. Accordingly, that law should be studied not only as to its law of obligations, but also in relation to its effect on the agreement to arbitrate. It should be noted, however, that because of the "autonomy" of the arbitration clause, it does not automatically follow that the proper law of the agreement applies to it. For example, in France the courts have ruled, in effect, that an arbitration agreement in an international contract is not governed by domestic law at all.

A dramatic example discussed in Chapter 3: Choosing the Place of Arbitration, is the approach of the Indian and Pakistani courts. Until 1996, the courts in both countries treated arbitration awards made in relation to contracts governed by Indian or Pakistani law as "domestic awards" subject to review by the local courts even if the place of arbitration was outside India or Pakistan. This enabled the party against whom enforcement was sought to seek to set aside the award on its merits, in a manner excluded by the New York Convention. An example of this was the *Sumitomo* case in which it was held that the procedural law of the arbitration (English law) ceased to apply when the proceedings before the arbitrators were concluded. The enforcement process was held to be subject to Indian law, the governing law of the contract. This kind of problem appears to have been cured in India by its Arbitration and Conciliation Act 1996, although not in Pakistan, where the old legislation remains in force.

National laws

It is wrong to assume that the choice of applicable law is immaterial if a detailed contract has been drafted, setting out the parties' rights and obligations *in extenso*. There are often gaps to be filled.

Moreover, some national laws contain mandatory provisions that add to the rights or obligations contained in the contract, or override explicit contractual stipulations. Some laws are particularly favourable to purchasers. Others allow an acknowledged debtor of a liquidated sum to suspend payment by seeking to set off a non-liquidated claim in court or arbitration proceedings. Some laws allow judges or arbitrators to revise contractual terms they find unreasonable, whilst others vigorously take the opposite position.

The idiosyncrasies of applicable national laws are often attenuated in international arbitrations by the following factors:

- most arbitration rules require the arbitral tribunal in all cases to take account of the terms of the contract and of trade usages;

- arbitration is founded in contract; arbitral tribunals are therefore reluctant to disregard contractual provisions, recognising that parties operating internationally are often less aware of the provisions of various foreign national laws than those of their home country, and that their legitimate expectations are best fulfilled if they are held to their bargain;

- the contract law of many countries has often been influenced by consumer transactions and other situations involving parties whose lack of sophistication understandably provokes legislators to protect them; such situations are far less prevalent with respect to international contracts involving large amounts of money and drafted by skilled negotiators.

Subject to identifying any particular characteristics of the kind indicated above, the interests of certainty usually require that the parties choose the national law of the country most closely associated with the transaction: or, alternatively, a neutral law with rules of contractual interpretation which are well developed and accessible to foreigners (preferably in the language of the contract). This choice will be respected by almost all developed arbitration systems. As stated in the UNCITRAL Model Law "the arbitral tribunal shall decide the dispute in accordance with such rules of law as are chosen by the parties as applicable to the substance of the dispute". The parties' choice is also explicitly upheld in arbitration rules such as those of the ICC (Article 17) the LCIA (Article 22.3) and UNCITRAL (Article 33(1)).

In the course of negotiations there is often a trade-off between a national law favoured by one party and a place of arbitration favoured by another. In such a situation, particular care should be taken to ensure that the place of arbitration is suitable for determining a dispute *governed by the national law so chosen*, bearing in mind mandatory rules of law under the umbrella of public policy or *ordre publique*: see Chapter 3 – Choosing the Place of Arbitration.

What if no substantive law is chosen?

In the absence of a law chosen by the parties to determine the substantive issues in any dispute, how will the arbitrators go about doing so?

Traditionally, the arbitrators would apply the conflict of laws rules of the place (or seat) of arbitration in order to determine the applicable law. Accordingly, an arbitral tribunal sitting in London would apply English conflict of laws rules even if neither party were English and the substance of the dispute had no connection with England. This solution met with understandable criticism since the place of arbitration was often chosen for its geographical convenience or neutrality, or may even have been imposed by an arbitral institution. Modern laws and arbitration rules now give the tribunal the freedom to apply the "rules of law which it determines to be appropriate" (e.g. Article 17 of the ICC Rules) – the so-called *voie directe* which does not require reference to any system of conflict of laws – or to select the conflict of laws rules which it considers applicable (e.g. Article 33 of the UNCITRAL Rules and s. 46(3) of the English Arbitration Act 1996).

Freed from the shackles of the conflict of laws rules of the place of arbitration, arbitrators naturally sought a generally acceptable set of rules for determining the applicable law. An important source was to be found in the 1980 Rome Convention on the Law Applicable to Contractual Obligations which, whilst not directly applicable to arbitration, may nevertheless be viewed as an expression of internationally agreed concepts. Broadly, the Convention provides that a contract shall be governed by the law chosen by the parties and that the choice must be made expressly or demonstrated with reasonable certainty. If no such choice is made, the contract is treated as being governed by the law of the country with which it is most closely connected.

General principles of law

The best hope of reaching an agreement on the substantive law is sometimes to avoid reference to a national law altogether and opt for "general principles of law". This approach should be adopted with caution.

General principles of law are frequently referred to in choice of law clauses, whether alone or in conjunction with some national system of law or as forming part of international trade law. Some important arbitral awards have been founded on general principles of law.

The problem, for the lawyer as much as for the businessman, is that general principles of law are just that, and not a developed code of law. The concepts that contracts must be obeyed *(pacta sunt servanda),* that good faith is important in commercial relationships, that a breach of a contractual commitment involves an obligation to make reparation, that a person should not enrich himself unjustly at the expense of another – and other, similar, principles – are a valuable source of law, but often do not provide definite answers to particular questions.

If general principles of law are to be referred to in a choice of law clause, then – because of their necessarily general nature – they are better used in conjunction with a defined system of national law. This creates a concurrence of laws, discussed below.

Common principles of national laws

In major contracts between parties operating in the international arena (often involving a state entity or highly political project), national pride sometimes results in complex applicable law clauses which prove difficult to apply in practice. Recent examples include the applicable law clause in the Channel Tunnel project where the contract was governed by "the principles common to both English law and French law and, in the absence of such common principles, by such general principles of international trade law as have been applied by national and international tribunals".

The authors have encountered an even more exotic clause in an oil contract specifying the applicable law as "the common principles of the laws of England and the Russian Federation and in default of such common principles, the laws of Alberta, Canada". Whilst such clauses may be expedient and raise interesting questions for comparative lawyers, they are likely to lead to increased costs and reduced certainty for the parties – and should be avoided where possible.

So how should this type of situation be resolved? In the event that each party refuses to accept the law of the other party, the solution may be to select a venue for the arbitration where the relevant substantive law is developed and accessible and agree that it governs the contract.

Concurrent laws

Where one party to a contract is a state or state agency, principles of international law (or alternatively the general principles of law) are often coupled with a national law, so as to create a separate system of concurrent laws. Public international law (or alternatively, the general principles of law) then acts as a regulator of the national law, ensuring that it does not fall below a minimum international standard.

The 1965 Washington Convention provides a striking example of this tendency in relation to disputes between states and foreign nationals in connection with disputes submitted to ICSID arbitration. Article 42(1) of the Convention provides that, in the absence of any express choice of law by the parties, an ICSID tribunal shall apply the law of the contracting state and "such rules of international law as may be applicable". The law of the contracting state is recognised as paramount within its own territory, but is nevertheless subjected to international control. In this way, international law sets a minimum standard which the arbitral tribunal is mandated to uphold in its award.

A further example is the Energy Charter Treaty. Article 26 sets out the dispute resolution procedures available under the Treaty. Article 26(2) provides that a dispute is to be decided in accordance with the Treaty and the applicable rules and principles of international law. The Treaty does not require the tribunal to consider any governing law specified in the investor-state contract in question, which may suggest that the tribunal should apply principles of international law exclusively, and not as a secondary or corrective source.

Clauses "freezing" the law

Contracts made between a state or state agency on the one hand and a private entity on the other are generally known as 'state contracts'. The private entity is often under considerable commercial pressure to agree that the law governing the contract shall be that of the state concerned. This raises the fear that the state party may subsequently use its legislative powers to alter the law, and hence the contractual regime, without the consent of the private party.

For example a state, having granted a concession to the private party to construct and run a railway, or to build and operate a gas liquefaction plant, might, once the operation is on stream, decree an increase of its share of revenue beyond that originally agreed, or levy taxes, or act in some other fashion that diminishes the return to the private party.

One technique sometimes used as a measure of protection against arbitrary legislation by the state party – at the extreme, nationalisation without compensation – is to couple the law of the state party with principles of international law (see above in relation to "Concurrent laws"). Another is that of 'freezing' the law of the state party. The relevant law is expressed to be the law in force at the date of the contract – thus avoiding the application of any subsequent change in the law to the detriment of the private party.

If freezing the law is unacceptable to the state party, an appropriate move in this direction might nevertheless be agreed in the form of a 'stabilisation clause' – under which the state party would, for instance, undertake that benefits granted under the contract would not be diminished by supervening legislative or regulatory changes.

Provisions of this kind may be worth considering in appropriate cases. However, there is considerable controversy as to whether a state can restrict its future legislative powers by means of a private contract, as opposed to a treaty. At best, the effect of such clauses may be to give a special right to compensation if the law is changed so as to affect adversely the private party's interests.

The *lex mercatoria*

The increasing complexity and internationalisation of modern trade and commerce have led some lawyers to conclude that what is needed to govern contractual relationships is not a particular national system of law but a modern law merchant. Such a law, it is said, would meet the requirements of international commerce in much the same way as the *lex mercatoria* met the requirements of traders living under the Roman Empire; or as enactments of customary law (such as the celebrated *Consulato del Mare)* met the needs of sailors and merchants in the Mediterranean in the 14th century.

This modern law merchant goes under various descriptions, including 'transnational law', 'the international law of contracts', 'international lex mercatoria' and 'international trade law'. Whatever the description, the purpose is clear; it is to regulate international commercial transactions by a uniform system of law.

The problem again, as with the concept of general principles of law, lies in the vagueness of the *lex mercatoria*. Nevertheless, arbitral tribunals have on occasion decided cases according to the *lex mercatoria* (equating it, perhaps, with concepts drawn from the arbitrators' own legal experience or commercial background) and their awards have been held to be in accordance with public policy and enforceable in both France and England, where significant test cases have arisen.

There is a risk, however, that until an acceptable body of rules has entered into currency in the international business community, the content of *lex mercatoria* is likely to differ according to the approach of the tribunal in each case and consequently lead to uncertainty in the outcome of the dispute. It thus becomes very difficult to advise on possible outcomes. Moreover, the prospects of early settlement may be hindered by the absence of a yardstick against which the likelihood of success can be measured.

The UNIDROIT Contract Principles

UNIDROIT, the International Institute for the Unification of Private Law, is based in Rome and has a Governing Council comprising academics and lawyers. UNIDROIT promotes the international harmonisation of law and seeks to establish guiding principles. It may well form the kernel of a new law merchant. Of particular importance is its "Principles of International Commercial Contracts", published in May 1994, which reflects some fourteen years of research and discussion by an international drafting committee. The Principles cover the formation, validity, interpretation and performance of international contracts. According to the preamble, they already form part of both "general principles of law" and *lex mercatoria*, although this claim will be established only by widespread acceptance and application of the Principles within the business and legal community.

The Principles expressly provide (in the preamble) for the possibility of parties agreeing to the application of the Principles to govern their contract. If parties wish to do so they should make clear that the Principles are to form the applicable "rules of law" of the contract to the exclusion of any national system. If not, the parties may find that the Principles bind them only to the extent that they do not conflict with the rules of national law otherwise applicable to the contract. Modern arbitration rules such as those of the ICC, LCIA and AAA all give the arbitrators a wide discretion to choose the appropriate "rules of law" and do not limit the choice to a national system of law.

The development of *lex mercatoria* is of particular relevance and importance to international arbitration which, by definition, transcends national boundaries and seeks to establish an international procedural order for the resolution of disputes in international trade and commerce. It is one (brave) step further towards establishing a set of international substantive legal norms for arbitration. It is a step which has the very highest judicial backing in remarks of a leading former judge of the English House of Lords, Lord Wilberforce, during the debate on the Bill which was to become the English Arbitration Act 1996:

> "I have always wished to see arbitration, as far as possible, and subject to statutory guidelines no doubt, regarded as a freestanding system, free to settle its own procedure and free to develop its own substantive law — yes, its substantive law..."

Trade usage

Article 17.2 of the ICC Rules expressly requires arbitrators to take account not only of the applicable law but also of the provisions of the contract and the relevant 'trade usages'. Similar provisions are to be found in Article 33(3) of the

UNCITRAL Arbitration Rules and Article 28(4) of the UNCITRAL Model Law. They may also be found in national arbitration laws such as the Netherlands Arbitration Act 1986 which provides that in all cases the arbitral tribunal "shall take into account any applicable trade usages".

Indeed, reference to trade usages as an aid to interpreting contractual provisions is commonplace in many legal systems. The UNIDROIT Principles also make express reference to international trade usages as relevant in the interpretation of contracts.

Trade usage must usually be established by evidence in any given case (unless it is common ground that the arbitral tribunal is familiar with the trade in question). However, organisations such as the ICC have been prominent in attempting to establish a commonly understood meaning for terms which are in frequent use in international trade contracts. Terms such as 'ex works', 'CIF' and 'FOB' are intended to establish a single international definition of certain rights and obligations. The extent of these rights and obligations is spelled out in an ICC booklet known as 'Incoterms' (or 'International Rules for the Interpretation of Trade Terms').

In much the same way, the ICC's Uniform Customs and Practice for Documentary Credits ("UCP"), which originated as long ago as 1933, have proved valuable in moving towards a single international standard for the interpretation of these important instruments of world trade. This will be further assisted by the 1997 ICC Rules for Documentary Credit Expertise which are aimed at the speedy and reliable resolution of disputes between banks concerning the application of the UCP.

These are but a few examples of the international standards and rules that emerge in any significant service, trade or industry which crosses national frontiers. Standard form contracts are commonplace in the shipping trade, in the commodity markets and in the oil industry. It is only a small step from the establishment of international terms and conditions to the establishment of uniform rules for the interpretation of these terms and conditions. If such rules are uniformly applied by many different national courts, or by arbitral tribunals, the basis is laid for the establishment of an international customary law created by merchants and traders.

Amiable composition and equity clauses

In cases where the parties have, for pragmatic reasons, chosen a law to govern the contract which is not the domestic law of either of them, the decision of an arbitral tribunal based squarely in fairness or equity may be preferable to one based on law, particularly where the contract provides for a long-term relationship. An equity clause may allow for the selection of arbitrators who are not lawyers but who are knowledgeable about the specific subject matter in dispute.

Furthermore, giving the arbitral tribunal power to act as *amiables compositeurs* may fit well in situations where the parties to a long-term agreement wish a third party to have the power to take account of new or changing circumstances in resolving future disputes. Authorising arbitrators to act as *amiables compositeurs* does not, however, necessarily give them power to fill gaps or revise the terms of the contract in respect of unforeseen developments. If required, it is best to confer such a power expressly in the arbitration clause or submission agreement. This is considered further in Chapter 7: Choosing Mechanisms to Deal with Specific Situations.

Such provisions are intended to produce a binding and enforceable award; but one which the arbitral tribunal may reach without applying strict legal principles, if the result would appear unjust. Some jurisdictions question the validity or international enforceability of awards made by way of *amiable composition*. England was, in the past, one such jurisdiction. However, even England has now embraced the idea by allowing arbitrators to decide disputes "in accordance with such other considerations as are agreed by [the parties] or determined by the tribunal" (section 46(1)(b) Arbitration Act 1996).

Most arbitration rules provide that the arbitral tribunal may decide the dispute as *amiables compositeurs* (or *ex aequo et bono*) only if the parties expressly agree: see, for example, ICC Rules Article 17.3, LCIA Rules Article 22.4 and UNCITRAL Rules Article 33(2).

It is almost impossible to frame a definition of the term *amiable composition* in a form which would be fully accepted by all authorities on the subject. (It is probably best understood in France, where it originated and is given express statutory recognition). However, the distinctive characteristic of arbitrators having power to act as *amiables compositeurs* is that they need not apply strict legal rules of interpretation to the obligations of the parties, contractual or otherwise, if they consider that a strict legal approach would lead to an inequitable result. In particular, *amiables compositeurs* may take a more flexible approach to the quantification of damages in order to reflect commercial fairness and reality, rather than regarding themselves as bound by rules of law governing standards of compensation.

It should be emphasised that equity in the context of *amiable composition* does not refer to any system of specific rules and remedies, as that term is understood in common law countries. It encompasses a looser and broader concept. An arbitral tribunal given powers of *amiable composition* is empowered to render a binding decision which seeks to reflect the expectations of the parties.

The powers of *amiables compositeurs* are not unlimited, nor should they be. They must observe due process in giving equality of treatment to the parties, and they are bound by rules of public policy as well as any applicable mandatory rules of law. Before agreeing to an *amiable composition* clause, the contract negotiator should ensure that the law of the proposed place of arbitration permits such a provision and that an award not based on substantive rules of law is enforceable.

3

Choosing the place of arbitration

One of the key decisions which has to be made when drafting the arbitration clause is as to the legal place or "seat" of the arbitration. When considering this issue, many contract negotiators tend to focus primarily on geographical neutrality. They also typically want a convenient venue – or at least a venue which is equally inconvenient for both parties – as well as cultural neutrality. Whilst these factors should be accorded some significance, two other considerations are paramount, namely:
– a favourable legal environment, and
– the enforceability of the award.

Provided these two legal criteria are satisfied, consideration should be given to practical matters such as geographical convenience for the parties, counsel and witnesses, and the availability of support services.

Contract negotiators should not leave the choice to fate – or, more accurately, the discretion of an arbitral institution. Institutions may select a place of arbitration which is geographically "neutral" but which imposes a legal and physical environment which neither party would have chosen freely.

Favourable legal environment

Not all countries are safe havens for international arbitration. Some cling to wide powers of judicial review. Others have unclear legislation. Yet others have apparently adequate legislation but their courts seem to misapply the law – for example by adopting an over-elastic interpretation of 'violation of public policy' as grounds for setting aside awards.

Legal systems allowing extensive judicial interference with arbitral awards should be avoided. When selecting an arbitration venue, care should be taken to ensure that the local courts will (i) enforce the arbitration agreement; (ii) not interfere unduly in the arbitral process; and (iii) respect the finality of the award, for example by giving effect to an agreement of the parties to restrict or exclude rights of appeal.

One of the cornerstones of international arbitration is the 1958 New York Convention on the Recognition and Enforcement of Foreign Arbitral Awards which provides for both the enforcement of arbitration agreements and the enforceability of arbitral awards (see below). Under Article 2 of the Convention, signatory states must stay (suspend) court proceedings brought in breach of the arbitration agreement and refer the parties to arbitration. Consequently, parties should avoid locating arbitrations in countries which are not signatories to the Convention. As there are now over 120 signatory states, this is not a particularly exclusive requirement. (Since Portugal's accession to the Convention in 1994, the only holdout in Europe is Albania although anomalies remain, as in the case of Brazil, which has not signed). The full list of New York Convention countries appears at Appendix 5.

Once it has been determined that the chosen place of arbitration is a signatory to the New York Convention, the local law should be reviewed to ascertain whether it gives rise to any concerns. In particular, consideration should be given to whether or not there is a right of appeal to the local courts, permitting such courts to interfere with the merits of awards. Interference with proceedings by granting injunctions should not be permitted. Local courts should be able to set aside the award only on procedural grounds such as want of jurisdiction or serious misconduct by the arbitrators.

Therefore, if there is a right of appeal to the local courts, it should be considered whether it can validly be excluded by agreement between the parties. If so, the adoption of the ICC, LCIA and AAA Rules will automatically exclude any rights of appeal. However, it should be noted that the UNCITRAL Rules do not expressly exclude rights of appeal and specific exclusion wording would need to be added.

Jurisdictions which require the parties' counsel, or the arbitrators, to be of local nationality and/or admitted to the local bar should also be avoided. The applicable law (or even the language) in an arbitration may not be that of the place of the arbitration and local counsel may not be qualified to argue the case. Parties want to be able to select their counsel and arbitrators from the widest possible pool of specialists and not be limited by unnecessarily restrictive rules.

This particular concern has had a negative effect on the suitability of some South East Asian countries as arbitral venues. However, the position is improving as a result of recent reforms (see below).

The UNCITRAL Model Law

One way to determine whether a particular jurisdiction is arbitration-friendly is to check whether the country in question has adopted the UNCITRAL Model Law on International Commercial Arbitration. The Model Law was adopted by the United Nations in 1985 aimed at establishing an internationally acceptable arbitration law which countries could enact with their own legislation, subject only to taking account of any special requirements or idiosyncrasies of their particular legal system. It has made a considerable impact, especially on those states which did not previously have a developed arbitration law.

In some cases it is difficult to determine whether a particular state has *fully* adopted the Model Law, as it may have enacted it with more or less significant amendments. For example, such amendments may permit anti-arbitration injunctions (as in India) or add substantive grounds for review (as in Egypt). Nevertheless, UNCITRAL has itself compiled a list of some 30 countries which have so far adopted the Model Law and this appears at Appendix 6.

The UNCITRAL Model Law is based upon the principle that the local courts in the place of arbitration should support, but not interfere with, the arbitral process. Some of its key features are as follows:

1. Courts must support the arbitral process by ordering a stay (suspension) of court proceedings brought in breach of a valid arbitration agreement, thereby reflecting the requirement of Article 2 of the New York Convention;

2. Parties may seek the assistance of the courts to obtain interim relief or bring evidence before the arbitral tribunal (e.g. by subpoena of documents or witnesses);

3. Any "inherent" jurisdiction of the courts to interfere in the arbitral process is excluded;

4. No person shall be precluded by reason of nationality from acting as an arbitrator;

5. Each party should receive equal treatment and be given a proper opportunity to present its case;

6. The role of the courts is limited to:
   - acting as an appointing authority where the parties' chosen appointment procedure fails (in practice, likely only in an *ad hoc* arbitration)
   - deciding upon any challenge concerning the impartiality or independence of arbitrators (also most common in an *ad hoc* arbitration)
   - deciding upon any challenge to the jurisdiction of the tribunal
   - deciding any application to set aside the award on the grounds of excess of jurisdiction, failure to give a party a proper opportunity to present its case, or violation of

public policy. The correction of errors of fact or law is beyond the powers of review by the courts.

Enforceability of awards

Most of the 120 or more states which have ratified or acceded to the New York Convention have adopted the so-called reciprocity reservation. That effectively means that the courts of that state will enforce an award under the Convention only if it has been made within the territory of another state which has also adhered to the New York Convention. The nationality of the parties is immaterial: it is the 'nationality' of the award that counts. Therefore, only New York Convention countries should normally be considered as suitable places to hold international arbitrations.

Other multilateral or bilateral treaties may also come into play, such as the European Convention on International Commercial Arbitration of 1961 or the Inter-American Convention on International Commercial Arbitration of 1975 (which has particular relevance for Brazil as a non-signatory of the New York Convention – see below).

As a general rule, a state which is a party to the New York Convention and which has adopted the Model Law will be a suitable place, or seat, of arbitration. However, it should be noted that there are many arbitration-friendly states which have their own developed arbitration laws (e.g. the leading arbitration venues of France, Sweden, Switzerland, the Netherlands, the USA and the UK) and so the adoption of the UNCITRAL Model Law certainly should not be regarded as providing the only answer.

Although tempting, it is inadvisable in a Guide such as this to seek to set out a list of acceptable arbitration venues and thereby provoke protests, justifiable or not, on the grounds of omission. However, some guidance as to the appropriateness of particular venues is provided by the frequency with which they are used for arbitrations. The ICC publishes annual statistics of places of ICC arbitration chosen by the parties or fixed by the ICC court. We set out below a non-exhaustive summary for the period 1992 to 1998. A crucial factor in the choice of the place of arbitration is the attitude of the local courts. The parties' interest in obtaining a reliable award is obvious; the ICC has an institutional stake in avoiding countries whose courts appear to be too ready to set aside its awards.

Based on the ICC statistics, France is the most frequently used venue in Western Europe, Singapore the most used in Asia (eclipsing Hong Kong), and the United States the most used in the Americas.

ICC statistics 1992–1998

Country	Chosen by parties or fixed by the ICC
Western Europe	France (187)
	Switzerland (143)
	United Kingdom (91)
	Austria (20)
	Sweden (18)
	Germany (28)
	Italy (11)
	Luxembourg (6)
	Netherlands (12)
	Belgium (9)
	Denmark (2)
Asia	Singapore (15)
	Hong Kong (6)
	India (11)
	Japan (3)
	Republic of Korea (2)

Country	Chosen by parties or fixed by the ICC
The Americas	USA (57)
	Canada (10)
	Mexico (5)
	Argentina (3)
	Ecuador (1)

Switzerland, Sweden and the Netherlands are typical neutral venues in the sense that they are chosen by parties whose nationality and contractual relationship have nothing whatsoever to do with the forum. Not surprisingly, all three have enacted progressive legislation to ensure that they may legitimately be perceived as safe places for international arbitration.

Given the relative size of their economies, Germany, Italy and Spain have remarkably seldom been accepted as venues for international arbitration. This is to be explained by arbitration laws and judicial attitudes perceived to be interventionist and outdated. The perception of Germany in this respect may be dramatically improved as the result of its lock-stock-and-barrel adoption of the Model Law in 1998.

The relatively low position of the United Kingdom in the Western Europe list (considering the importance of London as a trading and financial centre) is largely due to the fact that, historically, English arbitration law was considered unacceptable to international practitioners because of the availability of appeals to the court on questions of law.

The arbitration law of England and Wales (Scotland and Northern Ireland have separate legal systems) was radically overhauled by the passage of the Arbitration Act 1996, which has greatly improved the legal framework necessary to instil confidence in users of international arbitration. The new Act provides for certain mandatory provisions – such as the stay (suspension) of Court proceedings in favour of arbitration, the general duties of the tribunal and the parties, and the enforcement of awards – and a series of non-mandatory provisions in relation to which the parties may either "contract in" (e.g. the power of the tribunal to award interim relief) or "contract out" (e.g. the power of the tribunal to grant security for costs). The adoption of institutional rules, such as those of the ICC or the LCIA, will constitute an agreement of the parties for the purposes of the Act.

One point to note is the removal of the historical distinction between domestic and international arbitration and the special categories of maritime, insurance and commodities arbitration. Consequently, contrary to the earlier position, parties may now contract out of the right to appeal to the court on a point of law in domestic as well as international arbitrations and in these special areas. The 1994 case of *Ken-Ren* which concerned the power of the court to award security for costs against a non-resident claimant (and which had been heralded by some as the death knell of arbitration in England) has been overruled by the Act, which provides that the power to award security for costs rests solely with the arbitral tribunal, subject to the parties' agreement to the contrary. Now that these and other ghosts have been laid to rest, London's future as an international arbitral venue looks secure.

Practical considerations

Once the legal issues of the possibility of local court intervention and enforceability of the award are satisfactorily evaluated, the contract negotiator should not forget the practicalities of organising the arbitration if and when a dispute arises. The following matters in particular should be borne in mind:

— geographical convenience

If the contract is between parties located in jurisdictions a long way apart, consideration should be given to locating the arbitration in a neutral venue of equal convenience to both parties.

– availability of suitable arbitrators

It is desirable to choose a place of arbitration where there is an adequate pool of experienced arbitrators, especially since the sole or presiding arbitrator may be chosen for his or her understanding of the local procedural law. In some countries only a handful of arbitrators have experience of complex international disputes in a given area of specialisation or in a given language. With bad luck, they may all be eliminated by conflicts of interest or unavailability, in which case there is a risk of ending up with a mediocre tribunal.

– location of subject matter in dispute

If the contract might give rise to a technical dispute, it is likely that the arbitrators and the parties' counsel will wish to examine the subject matter of the dispute (such as the relevant technical plant or building). Consideration should, in such a case, be given to locating the arbitration in a venue close to the subject matter of the contract.

– location of witnesses

If potential witnesses are mainly located in a particular geographic area, choosing a venue either close to or within that area is likely to reduce cost and enhance the likelihood of attendance.

– availability of support services

Contract negotiators should ensure that there are appropriate facilities available in the proposed arbitration venue, including accommodation, hearing rooms, stenographic and secretarial services, fax, telephone and possibly videoconferencing if key witnesses may be unable to attend in person.

Meetings and hearings outside the place of arbitration

Most arbitration rules provide a considerable degree of flexibility in where meetings and hearings may take place. Article 20(2) of the UNCITRAL Model Law itself states that "the arbitral tribunal may, unless otherwise agreed by the parties, meet at any place it considers appropriate for consultation among its members, for hearing witnesses, experts or the parties, or for the inspection of goods, other property or documents." Similar provisions may be found in the ICC, LCIA, UNCITRAL and AAA Rules.

It is therefore perfectly appropriate for tribunals to meet outside the place of the arbitration, for example in order to inspect property or hear a particular witness.

Regional issues

There are a number of countries where particular idiosyncrasies have arisen which may trap the unwary contract negotiator. Whilst we do not aim to be exhaustive in addressing such concerns, and they may improve in time, we draw attention to some of the more important issues which have arisen when selecting an arbitral venue in certain countries outside the mainstream. As many of these elements are regional in character, we have addressed them accordingly.

(a) Eastern Europe

Russia

There are considerable practical difficulties in enforcing "foreign" arbitration awards in Russia. In relation to the many projects located within Russia, it may sometimes be preferable, although counter-intuitive, to choose a place of arbitration in Russia itself. Whilst this may itself entail difficulties in enforcing the award outside Russia, a foreign party who elects to arbitrate a dispute with a Russian party before the International Commercial Arbitration Court at the Chamber of Commerce of the Russian Federation (*ICAC*) may benefit from the special statutory interlocutory powers of the President of the Court to secure claims (see Chapter 5: Choosing the Rules). This may prove particularly valuable in the event of competing claims. Bearing in mind Russia's adoption of the UNCITRAL Model Law and the ability of parties to nominate an arbitrator of their choice, arbitration in Russia under the auspices of ICAC may be considered as an alternative to institutional arbitration elsewhere for Russian-related disputes. However, the by-word is caution: due to the unpredictability of rulings of the local courts and the uncertain prospects of enforcement, specialist advice should always be obtained.

(b) The Indian Sub-Continent

India

Prior to the passage of the Arbitration and Conciliation Act 1996, a number of concerns arose from arbitrating in India or arbitrating elsewhere an agreement governed by Indian law. First, the courts in India had wide-ranging powers of intervention in the course of the arbitral process, which enabled determined defendants and their imaginative lawyers to stall the proceedings at every stage. Secondly, the Foreign Awards (Recognition and Enforcement) Act 1961 which was intended to implement the New York Convention, had in one instance quite the opposite effect. Section 9(b) of that law provided that any award made on an arbitration agreement governed by the law of India was not a foreign award and could not therefore be enforced in accordance with the provisions of the New York Convention. As a result, an arbitration award made in London in respect of an agreement governed by Indian law could be reviewed by the courts in India as if it were a domestic award (as in the notorious *Singer* case). These problems appear to have been solved by the 1996 Act, although evidence of its application by the Indian courts is awaited.

Pakistan

Pakistan has suffered from exactly the same problem as India. Section 9(b) of its own international arbitration statute, the Arbitration (Protocol and Convention) Act 1937, which is still in force, treats foreign awards made pursuant to agreements (and agreements to arbitrate) governed by Pakistani law as domestic awards and therefore subject to review on the merits by the courts in Pakistan. It is therefore vital for the contract negotiator to ensure that the agreement to arbitrate is expressly governed by a different law, for example, the law of the place of arbitration, in order to avoid such review of the award. It should also be noted that Pakistan has signed but not ratified the New York Convention, although new legislation is planned to provide for the recognition and enforcement of foreign arbitral awards.

(c) Asia-Pacific

China

China ratified the New York Convention in 1987, subject to the reciprocity and commercial reservations. Arbitrations held in China may be conducted under the auspices of:

(i) the China International Economic Trade Commission (CIETAC) for cases involving trade, investment and other commercial disputes;

(ii) the Chinese Maritime Arbitration Commission (CMAC), with regard to maritime disputes; or

(iii) one of various domestic arbitration commissions.

Parties arbitrating international disputes within China almost invariably do so according to the rules of CIETAC, which has a virtual (but not complete) monopoly over arbitrations conducted in China. This is because:

(i) there is no provision for *ad hoc* arbitration taking place in China in the Arbitration Law (although the Chinese courts will recognise clauses providing for foreign *ad hoc* arbitrations taking place outside China); and

(ii) although the PRC became a member of the ICC in November 1994, there is no clear mechanism for conducting ICC or indeed other institutional arbitrations in China and enforcing such awards.

The governing body of CIETAC is its Arbitration Commission which (like the ICC) does not decide cases, but rather administers arbitrations according to its rules. The Arbitration Commission maintains a single panel of arbitrators from which all arbitrators appointed to act in CIETAC arbitrations must be selected.

The latest version of CIETAC's rules came into effect on 10 May 1998. Hearings tend to be short and informal, with emphasis being placed upon discovery of the facts rather than legal analysis. Lengthy hearings involving multiple sessions over a period of months are therefore almost unheard of. There is no objection, either under CIETAC's rules or according to Chinese law, to foreign lawyers representing parties in CIETAC arbitration.

In 1996 domestic arbitration commissions were authorised to accept foreign-related cases, although their rules are less sophisticated than those of CIETAC which were specially drafted to meet the needs of international arbitration. Further, it is questionable whether foreign lawyers may appear before domestic arbitration commissions; the choice of arbitrators is more limited than CIETAC; and it is not clear whether an award made by a domestic tribunal concerning a foreign-related case would be enforceable in the usual way in a New York Convention country.

Contract negotiators involved in transactions with Chinese counterparties where the place of arbitration is to be within the PRC should therefore ensure that arbitration clauses refer to CIETAC arbitration rather than to arbitration before domestic arbitration commissions: see Chapter 5 – Choosing the Rules.

Hong Kong

Hong Kong has long held the premier position amongst South East Asian venues for international arbitrations due mainly to a modern UNCITRAL-based law, its accession to the New York Convention and the availability of highly skilled local professionals and excellent facilities.

The transfer of sovereignty over Hong Kong from the UK to China on 1 July 1997 has not affected Hong Kong's position as a venue for international arbitration, with the important (but possibly temporary) exception of China disputes.

Prior to 1 July 1997, a large number of China disputes were resolved by international arbitration in the territory. Awards made in Hong Kong were enforceable in China as foreign awards under the New York Convention with its limited grounds for refusal of recognition and enforcement. After the handover, there was a growing concern that in spite of the "one country, two systems" pledge, a Hong Kong award would be treated as a domestic award in China (and vice-versa), thus enabling the party against whom enforcement is sought to invoke a much wider range of grounds on which to challenge enforcement.

In November 1998, the Hong Kong Secretary for Justice announced that the relevant authorities in China and Hong Kong had reached agreement regarding the reciprocal enforcement of arbitral awards between the Hong Kong SAR and mainland China. In summary, the agreement (which has not yet been signed or reflected in appropriate legislation) seeks to preserve the pre-handover practice, such that:

(i) amending legislation in Hong Kong will provide that PRC arbitral awards may be enforced in the same way as New York Convention awards in Hong Kong (whilst it was initially thought that this would only cover awards rendered by CIETAC and CMAC, recent reports suggest that the relevant focus will be whether the award falls within the New York Convention, rather than on the body which rendered the award);

(ii) in the PRC, the Supreme People's Court will issue a notice on the enforcement of Hong Kong awards which will provide that they may be enforced in accordance with the provisions of Chinese law relating to the enforcement of New York Convention awards;

(iii) the agreement will have retrospective effect, such that:
   (a) a Hong Kong award made after 1 July 1997 may be enforced in China if the application is submitted within 6 months after the date of commencement of the agreement;
   (b) where enforcement of a PRC award has been refused in Hong Kong, applications can be re-submitted within a time period to be determined; and
   (c) enforcement of arbitral awards made after the commencement of the new arrangement will follow the limitation period of the place of enforcement.

Singapore

Following a decision of the Singapore High Court in 1988 which determined that only Singapore lawyers could appear as counsel in arbitrations taking place in Singapore, the position was improved by an amendment to the Singapore Legal Profession Act in 1992. Foreign lawyers may now appear in arbitration proceedings in Singapore provided either that the law applicable to the dispute is not Singapore law or, if Singapore law does apply, that a Singapore lawyer appears jointly with the foreign lawyer.

This relaxation of the foreign counsel rule, together with the introduction of the Singapore International Commercial Arbitration Act 1994 (based on the Model Law), have boosted Singapore's popularity and acceptability as an international arbitration venue. No doubt influenced also by the uncertainties over the future of Hong Kong, Singapore hosted 12 ICC arbitrations in 1997, twice the number held in Hong Kong. The nascent Singapore International Arbitration Centre has handled over 300 arbitrations since its foundation in 1990.

Japan

The development of international arbitration in Japan has been seriously hampered by a local prohibition on foreign lawyer representation. Until 1 September 1996, parties to international arbitrations taking place in Japan were, under the provisions of the Special Measures Law Concerning the Handling of Legal Business by Foreign Lawyers (the Foreign Lawyers Law), able to instruct only lawyers admitted to practise domestic law in Japan ("Bengoshi").

The law of 1 September 1996 added new provisions to the Foreign Lawyers Law including a new definition of "international arbitration case":

> "... a civil case in which the place of arbitration is Japan and in which all or any of the parties have or has an address, main office or head office in a foreign country."

This new law therefore permits foreign lawyers (defined as those registered in Japan or retained from the foreign countries in which they practise) to represent parties in an "international arbitration case" even where the contracts or matters in dispute are governed by Japanese law or the procedure is influenced by Japanese civil litigation procedures. This amendment should ensure that more international arbitrations are brought before the Japan Commercial Arbitration Association (JCAA). Indeed, in 1997, the ICC Court fixed a

Japanese place of arbitration for the first time and the JCAA has now handled more than 10 international arbitrations in a year.

Malaysia

As a country with a common law tradition and a largely English speaking professional community, Malaysia has been highlighted as a serious contender to host international arbitrations in South East Asia. The Malaysian government has promoted this role by establishing and financing the Kuala Lumpur Regional Centre for Arbitration and by excluding certain arbitrations from the less than satisfactory Malaysian Arbitration Act of 1952, namely those held under the UNCITRAL Rules, as applied by the Kuala Lumpur Regional Centre, or the ICSID Rules. Such arbitrations would appear to be conducted in a legal vacuum with no statutory or common law underpinning: there is accordingly no power of review of awards made in accordance with these rules, even for misconduct.

Some may consider such a *laissez faire* approach worrying but others may consider it desirable in a region where the courts have historically taken too close an interest in the arbitral procedure. The most important point is to ensure that any clause providing for arbitration in Malaysia specifies the UNCITRAL Rules, as applied by the Kuala Lumpur Regional Centre for Arbitration, or the ICSID Rules in order to avoid the vagaries of the old law. Unlike Singapore and Japan, foreign representation has never been an issue and the exclusive rights of representation by locally qualified lawyers enshrined in the Legal Profession Act 1976 do not extend to arbitrations.

(d) Latin America

Until recently, many Latin American countries were openly hostile to international arbitration and arbitration clauses

41

often did not bind either party, each of whom would remain free to seek a judicial remedy unless they entered into a post-dispute submission agreement. This approach has changed radically and many countries have recently adopted new arbitration laws (e.g. Brazil, Colombia, Costa Rica, Ecuador, Guatemala, Mexico, Peru and Venezuela) or are currently in the process of adopting such new laws (Argentina and Chile) in order to provide more arbitration-friendly environments. However, the process is slow and, until further progress has been made, practical experience suggests that parties should avoid locating their arbitrations in the region. The main exception is Mexico which adopted the UNCITRAL Model Law some years ago and has a core of experts in the field. Mexico is the Latin American jurisdiction of choice for the ICC. Colombia and Peru also offer acceptable arbitration regimes, the former based on the French Code of Civil Procedure and the latter upon the UNCITRAL Model Law.

Inevitably, parties may be forced by reason of their negotiating position to accept a place of arbitration in the region, in which case one of the Model Law jurisdictions should be chosen where possible. The following countries also merit special comment:

Argentina

There is some case law of the Argentine Supreme Court indicating that the principles of the UNCITRAL Model Law should be followed in the case of international arbitration. However, pending passage of the new Argentine law (the bill is based on the Model Law) the existing law is antiquated and forbids non-Argentine nationals from sitting as arbitrators.

Chile

Chile's current law forbids non-Chileans from sitting as arbitrators, which greatly restricts the possible pool of suitably qualified and experienced arbitrators. Its law is also under review although the current bill does not adopt the Model Law and retains this nationality limitation (subject to displacement by express agreement of the parties).

Brazil

Brazil is the largest of the world's economies not to be a party to the New York Convention. This is a major disincentive to arbitrating in Brazil, since most states which have signed the New York Convention only agree to enforce awards on a reciprocal basis (see above and Appendix 5) and may legitimately refuse to enforce a Brazilian award. Brazil is, however, a party to the Panama Convention, a sister treaty sponsored by the Organisation of American States which ensures the mutual recognition and enforcement of arbitral awards across the Americas. Although the 1996 Arbitration Law states that all foreign awards will be enforced in Brazil, the contract negotiator should, if a contract involves a Brazilian party, aim to fix the place of arbitration in the United States (or other Latin American state such as Mexico) in order to have the added protection of the international enforcement regime.

Colombia

The Supreme Court decision mentioned in the first edition of this work – which interpreted the Constitution as requiring all arbitrators in arbitrations taking place in Colombia to be of Colombian nationality – has been overtaken by a 1996 law on international arbitration. This law now expressly permits foreigners to be named as arbitrators in international arbitrations.

Costa Rica

Costa Rica has recently passed new legislation, based loosely on the UNCITRAL Model Law and is in the process of establishing an international arbitration centre in conjunction with the American Chamber of Commerce. The new law leaves it unclear whether non-Costa Rican arbitrators may be appointed and all proceedings must be conducted in Spanish. However, there are moves to make amendments to these provisions to bring them in line with modern international practice.

4

Choosing the language of the arbitration

The very nature of international arbitration means that there is rarely a language common to all the parties, their representatives and the arbitrators. Nevertheless, the choice of the language of the arbitration is often ignored in arbitration clauses, risking leaving the parties and the arbitrators to determine the issues in an arbitral Tower of Babel overpopulated by translators and interpreters.

The issue is an important one: translation and interpretation are inevitably inexact sciences and legal concepts easily explainable in one language may become an awkward mixture of language and approximations in another. The differences in the world's legal systems ensure that many concepts of civil law do not translate neatly into the language of common lawyers, and vice versa.

The risks of misunderstanding and inappropriate translation of legal concepts from one culture to another increases the importance of having a three member tribunal where the dispute involves parties from more than one linguistic and legal culture (see Chapter 6: Choosing the Arbitrators). This should not, however, be thought of as a substitute for a considered choice of the language of the arbitration at the time of drafting the contract, having regard to such matters as the language of the contractual and other documents and the mother tongue of likely witnesses.

If the parties fail to choose the language of the arbitral proceedings, the main institutional rules will seek to fill the gap. The ICC Rules (Article 16) give the tribunal a wide discretion to decide the language (or languages) of the arbitration, "due regard being given to all relevant circumstances, including the language of the contract". Likewise, the UNCITRAL Rules give the tribunal complete discretion to determine the language (or languages) to be used in the proceedings.

The LCIA Rules (Article 17) recognise the need for an "initial language of the arbitration" pending the formation of the tribunal. Unless the parties have agreed otherwise in writing, such initial language "shall be" the language of the arbitration agreement. Where the arbitration agreement is written in more than one language, the LCIA Court decides which language will be the initial language of the arbitration. Once the tribunal has been established, the tribunal has a wide discretion to determine the definitive language (or languages) of the arbitration after giving the parties an opportunity to make written comments and taking into account the initial language of the arbitration and any other matter it may consider appropriate.

The AAA Rules (Article 14) create a presumption in favour of the language(s) of the documents containing the arbitration agreement, subject to the power of the tribunal to determine otherwise based upon "the contentions of the parties and the circumstances of the arbitration". This presumption is also reflected in the WIPO Rules.

It is to be observed that all of the major sets of rules recognise the possibility of having more than one language of the arbitration (this being only partially true for the LCIA which deals with the issue of the "initial language" of the arbitration prior to the formation of the arbitral tribunal). Although this may add considerably to the cost of the proceedings, it ensures that the tribunal has the power to recognise and deal with the difficulties that one party might have in properly presenting its case in a foreign language.

The fundamental problem with each of the main sets of arbitration rules is the extremely wide discretion granted to the tribunal to determine the language of the arbitration. Very little guidance is given, subject to varying degrees of importance attached to the language of the contract. Nearly two-thirds of contracts submitted to ICC arbitration are drafted in English (as opposed to some 20% in French, the next most likely possibility). This predominance of the use of English is implicitly recognised in the LCIA Rules which prevent a non-participating or defaulting party from complaining "if communications to and from the Registrar and the arbitration proceedings are in English" (Article 17.1). The aim of this provision was to prevent a defaulting party delaying the proceedings by suggesting that his rights had been infringed by not being permitted to plead in his own language even though the underlying contract was written in English, which is widely recognised as the *lingua franca* of modern international commerce.

Another problem arises when considering the use of the rules of one of the many regional arbitration centres (see Chapter 5: Choosing the Rules). Although the parties remain free to select the language of the arbitration, the default mechanism may favour the local language. Such is the case with arbitrations held under the rules of ICAC in Moscow and CIETAC in China.

The best solution is to specify the language in the arbitration clause. When choosing the language of the arbitration, consideration should be given to the applicable law of the contract, the place of arbitration, the language of the contract, the language of the other principal documents, the mother tongue of likely witnesses and the likely availability of suitable arbitrators and/or counsel who could operate easily in the language of the arbitration.

5

Choosing the rules

Institutional or *ad hoc*?

Given the widespread acceptance of a small number of arbitral institutions and their published rules, it is not surprising that parties generally refer to them in accordance with the institution's recommended clause (or at least attempt to do so) rather than expend the necessary time, energy and expense in developing an *ad hoc* procedure. However, to suggest that the only appropriate way forward is to avoid *ad hoc* arbitration altogether (and merely choose between institutions) would oversimplify the issue.

Ad hoc rules

The principal benefit of an *ad hoc* arbitration agreement is that it can be tailored to the precise needs of the parties and the type of dispute likely to arise under a particular contract. It may also (at least superficially) appear cheaper as it does away with the administration costs of institutional arbitration.

In reality, the negotiation of a properly drafted *ad hoc* clause is a major task and one that should not be undertaken lightly without specialist advice. In the context of the contractual negotiations it is unlikely that the parties will want to devote the time and effort involved in establishing a workable and appropriate procedure for resolving disputes not yet anticipated, let alone identified.

Time and money can be saved by adopting or adapting rules of procedure which have been specially developed for *ad hoc* arbitrations. The best known are the UNCITRAL Rules, adopted in 1976 by the United Nations Commission on International Trade Law. Parties should not, however, seek to adapt the main institutional rules (such as those of the ICC or LCIA) for use in an *ad hoc* arbitration. The frequent references to the role of the institution in question make such a makeshift solution generally unworkable.

In the rare case of a truly *ad hoc* arbitration, the framework of the procedure should be set out fully but parties should avoid establishing every detail of the arbitral procedure as this is best left to be decided once a dispute has arisen. The key elements to include in such a clause are those governing the procedure to be followed, at least until the arbitral tribunal is established, including how the arbitration is to be commenced, an appointment procedure for the arbitrators, a timetable for an initial exchange of pleadings (to enable the parties and the arbitrators to understand the parameters of the dispute) and the finality (i.e. non appealability) of the award. A suggested all-purpose *ad hoc* clause is set out at Appendix 2.

The principal disadvantage of an *ad hoc* arbitration agreement is that its effectiveness depends in practice upon the voluntary co-operation of the parties to agree procedures at a time when they are already in dispute. If a party fails to co-operate, a number of time-consuming and expensive challenges may need to be made to the appropriate national court, for example, in relation to the appointment of arbitrators or the resolution of questions of jurisdiction. Whilst this may depend to some extent on the venue of the arbitration (e.g. under the English Arbitration Act, there are a number of default provisions; under French law, there are hardly any), these are matters which are likely to be dealt with more rapidly and effectively through an institutional structure. Furthermore, the strict time limits for the initial stages of the arbitration in the main institutional rules ensure that the arbitration is "up and running" in a much shorter time than its *ad hoc* equivalent.

The costs that may be saved by not involving an arbitral institution may therefore be illusory in the light of the additional delays in establishing the tribunal, the potential costs of going to court if faced with a recalcitrant party and the additional administrative burdens placed upon the tribunal once the arbitration is underway.

Institutional arbitration

Institutional arbitration is sometimes described as "administered" or "supervised" arbitration, although the degree of administration varies greatly from one institution to another.

This type of arbitration has many advantages and is generally preferred for international proceedings. The rules of prominent and well-established arbitral institutions such as the ICC, the LCIA and the AAA have benefited from the trial-and-error of practical application over many years. All three sets of rules have recently undergone major revisions in consultation with experienced practitioners – the new ICC and LCIA rules taking effect from 1 January 1998 and the revised AAA international rules from 1 April 1997. Each of the institutions distributes its rules in booklet form, free of charge, and they may be obtained by contacting the secretariat in each case (see Appendix 8 for details).

Most arbitral institutions provide trained staff and a governing body to administer the arbitration and to advise users. They ensure that the arbitral tribunal is appointed; that the basis of remuneration of the arbitrators is established; that advance payments are made in respect of the fees and expenses of the arbitrators; that time limits prior to the formation of the arbitral tribunal are observed. In an *ad hoc* arbitration these matters must be dealt with by the tribunal itself or an administrative secretary appointed by the tribunal.

The costs involved in using institutional arbitration vary greatly between institutions and may be based upon the amount in dispute (*ad valorem*), as is favoured by the ICC, or upon the time engaged on a particular matter, as provided by the LCIA and AAA.

The international acceptability of arbitral institutions

Once a party has decided in favour of institutional arbitration it must decide which institution should be used.

The last two decades have witnessed a proliferation of new arbitral institutions, mostly created along regional or industry lines. Many of the new regional institutions are aimed at enhancing the status of the city or region in question as a centre for commerce rather than addressing any real business need and, as a result, have often struggled to establish a viable caseload. This creates a vicious circle – parties do not insert arbitration clauses providing for arbitration under a new institution's rules due to the absence of practical experience or fear of the institution's lack of permanence; consequently the institution is unable to acquire the practical experience and viability necessary to ensure its permanence. As a result, few of the new institutions have acquired the critical mass necessary to guarantee their future or to instil sufficient peace of mind for the contract negotiator to make reference to their rules.

There are three principal arbitration institutions which have acquired a genuinely international vocation: the International Court of Arbitration of the ICC (based in Paris), the LCIA (based in London) and the American Arbitration Association (headquartered in New York). Reference to the rules of these institutions in the arbitration clause satisfies the need to ensure the permanence of the institution and will invoke a modern set of rules, all recently revised, which are specially devised and adapted to suit the international arbitral process.

The ICC

The International Court of Arbitration of the ICC (the ICC Court) was founded in 1923 and has since administered over 10,000 international arbitration cases. Its rules have been fully revised after extensive worldwide consultation and the new rules came into effect for arbitrations commenced after 1 January 1998.

The ICC Court does not actually decide disputes but appoints arbitral tribunals to deal with them. In 1998 the ICC Court comprised 68 members from 57 countries. During 1998 some 466 arbitrations were commenced under the new rules, involving parties and arbitrators from over 100 countries and with places of arbitration in 41 countries as diverse as Argentina and the UAE.

Through the unique procedures of the Terms of Reference and the scrutiny of awards, ICC arbitration is the most comprehensively supervised of the main arbitration systems. As a result it is often criticised as bureaucratic, interventionist and expensive. However, this degree of supervision and the institutional cachet of the ICC do appear in practice to enhance the enforceability of ICC awards.

Administration and Arbitrators' Fees

The following examples are given by the ICC in order to illustrate the calculation of the ICC's administrative expenses and the fees and expenses of the arbitrator(s), in all cases *ad valorem* by reference to the amount in dispute.

Example 1

The total amount of claims and counter-claims is US$ 1,000,000; the controversy is to be settled by a sole arbitrator. The advance on costs might be fixed as follows:

- administrative expenses   US$ 16,800
- estimated arbitrator's fees   US$ 32,375
  (minimum US$11,250/
  maximum US$ 53,500)
- expenses (travel, hotel, meeting rooms etc.) US$ 4,825

                          TOTAL   US$ 54,000

To sum up, for a dispute of US$ 1 million, settled by a single arbitrator, the advance on costs may amount to some US$ 54,000, that is 5.4% of the amount in dispute.

Example 2

The total amount of claims and counter-claims is US$25,000,000; the case is to be settled by three arbitrators.

- administrative expenses   US$ 42,800
- estimated arbitrators' fees (US$ 98,875 x 3) US$ 296,625
  (per arbitrator: minimum US$ 36,250/
  maximum US$ 161,500)
- expenses (travel, hotel, meeting rooms etc.) US$ 15,557

                          TOTAL   US$ 355,000

To sum up, for a dispute of US$ 25 million, the advance on costs may amount to US$ 355,000, that is 1.4% of the amount in dispute.

Provisional Advance on Costs

Under the 1998 Rules, the Secretary General of the ICC may request the Claimant to pay a provisional advance in an amount intended to cover the costs of the arbitration until the Terms of Reference have been finalised (Article 30(1)). Appendix III to the Rules suggests that this amount should not normally exceed the amount obtained by adding together the administrative expenses and likely arbitrators' fees and expenses incurred with regard to the drafting of the Terms of Reference. Although this advance is credited to the Claimant's share of the definitive advance on costs (which will be fixed by the ICC Court), it may place an additional financial burden on the Claimant at the initial stages of a claim. If, for example, the Claimant pays its share of the definitive advance and the Respondent refuses to pay, the Claimant will be required to pay on behalf of the Respondent in order for the arbitration to proceed, e.g. by posting a bank guarantee.

The LCIA

The LCIA (now formally to be known only by its acronym rather than its former name "The London Court of International Arbitration")[1] is the oldest of the internationally significant institutions, founded in 1892. The institution was comprehensively internationalised and rejuvenated in 1985 when a new set of rules was promulgated. Those rules have themselves been the subject of a major revision culminating in new rules which came into effect for arbitrations commenced after 1 January 1998.

The Arbitration Court of the LCIA (which, like the Court of the ICC, does not decide disputes but selects arbitrators to

---

[1] The name was changed in order to avoid any misunderstanding as to the significance of the word "London" and to promote the LCIA's international reach.

do so) consists of a President, seven Vice-Presidents and up to 29 other members. The Court has a genuinely international vocation: its current President is Canadian and his predecessor is German. Its seven Vice Presidents represent six different nationalities. No more than one quarter of the members of the Court may be British nationals and the 29 current members of the Court represent 18 nationalities in all. The LCIA has also formed Users' Councils in Europe, North America, Asia-Pacific and Africa and is in the course of establishing a Users' Council for Latin America. Arbitrations under its rules may be held anywhere in the world although, in the absence of a contractual choice, the place or "seat" of the arbitration will be London unless the LCIA Court determines otherwise in the light of all relevant factors.

In 1998, 63 new arbitrations were commenced under the new rules (plus 7 LCIA administered arbitrations under the UNCITRAL Rules) involving parties of 23 different nationalities and arbitrators of 15 different nationalities.

Since 1 January 1998, a registration fee of £1,500 is payable for commencing the arbitration. The administrative costs of the LCIA are based on time spent by the LCIA staff plus a percentage applied to the tribunal's fees, plus expenses. There are hourly fee rates of £150 for the Registrar or deputy and £75 for the Secretariat, plus an additional charge of 5% of the fees of the tribunal.

The fee rates for arbitrators in an LCIA arbitration normally range from £800 to £2,000 per working day. In exceptional cases, these figures can be higher or lower provided the fees are fixed by the LCIA Court following consultation with the arbitrators and provided the parties have expressly agreed to the fees.

The AAA

Whilst the American Arbitration Association ("AAA") is geared principally to servicing the US domestic arbitration market, it is handling an increasing number of international cases due to the number and strength of US businesses operating in the international arena.

In March 1991 the AAA first adopted a set of rules expressly for use in international arbitrations and a revised version was promulgated in 1997 for use in arbitrations commenced after 1 April 1997. The Rules are loosely based on the UNCITRAL Arbitration Rules. In the course of 1996, the AAA substantially restructured the way in which it administers international arbitrations by establishing the International Center for Dispute Resolution in New York, which administers all AAA international arbitrations regardless of the AAA office in which they were filed. During 1998, the International Center received a total of almost 400 cases involving parties from a total of 49 countries.

The AAA operates an *ad valorem* administrative filing fee structure. As from 1 April 1997, filing fees range from $500 for a claim of up to $10,000 to $7,000 for a claim of $5,000,000 (fees for higher claims are subject to negotiation). Additional administrative charges are based upon the number of days for the hearing ($150 per day before a single arbitrator and $250 per day before a three arbitrator panel).

Under the International Rules, AAA arbitrators are compensated on the basis of time spent on the case, taking into account their normal rates of compensation and the size and complexity of the case. The administrator arranges an appropriate hourly or daily rate, in consultation with the parties and the arbitrators themselves.

ICSID

The International Centre for the Settlement of Investment Disputes (ICSID) was established by the Washington Convention of 1965 and seeks to promote the settlement of investment disputes by means of two different procedures – arbitration and conciliation. It was established as an international method of settling disputes involving investments between contracting states and nationals of other states. In order to use the ICSID procedure, three conditions must first be fulfilled:

(a) the parties must agree that their dispute be submitted to ICSID arbitration;

(b) the dispute must be between a contracting state and a national of another contracting state;

(c) the dispute must be a legal dispute arising directly out of an investment. Although the term "investment" is not defined in the Convention, in practice it as been taken to include investment by the provision of services and technology as well as more traditional forms of capital investment.

As noted in Chapter Two: Choosing the Applicable Law, ICSID arbitration is governed by international law rather than by national law. The Washington Convention provides that each contracting state is to recognise awards as binding and all awards are enforceable within contracting states, without review under the relevant national law.

There is however, an internal review procedure established under the ICSID arbitration rules. An application for the interpretation, revision or annulment of an ICSID award may be made to the Secretary General of ICSID. If an annulment is sought, an *ad hoc* committee of three persons is appointed to consider the application. If the award is consequently annulled, in whole or in part, either party may request that the dispute be re-submitted to another arbitral tribunal.

Since contracts signed directly by a state are relatively infrequent, ICSID's caseload has historically been modest, seldom exceeding half a dozen cases in any year. Recently, the pace has quickened due to a new phenomenon: the proliferation of investment promotion laws and bilateral investment treaties which grant direct rights to investors to seek arbitration against states who have allegedly violated those laws or treaties – even if the investors have signed no contract with the relevant state. Many such laws or treaties refer to ICSID arbitration (see also the discussion of treaty arbitration in Chapter 7: Choosing Mechanisms to Deal with Specific Situations).

The PCA

The Permanent Court of Arbitration, which has its bureau at the Peace Palace in The Hague, was established in 1899 to deal with disputes involving states. Very few cases have in fact been submitted to the PCA.

The PCA is nevertheless of interest to practitioners for two reasons. First, in keeping with its original purposes to facilitate the resolution of disputes involving states, it has on a number of occasions made its first-rate facilities available so long as at least one of the parties to the dispute is a state or state organisation. Secondly, the PCA's Secretary-General has the important role of designating appointing authorities under the UNCITRAL Arbitration Rules where the parties have failed to choose such an appointing authority by agreement. Furthermore, their Rules were reformed in October 1992 to enable the PCA to expand its activities. The distinctive feature of the PCA is that, like UNCITRAL, it does not itself administer arbitrations.

Regional and national institutions

Apart from the main international institutions there are a number of important regional and national or nationally-based arbitration institutions which should be considered whenever a dispute arises in a particular geographical area. Special care should be taken in selecting some of the less well-known and internationally acceptable institutions. Some, such as the ICAC in Moscow, have special statutory powers and others, such as CIETAC in China may effectively be granted a special (or even monopoly) status for the conduct of international arbitrations in the particular country. Yet others, such as the Kuala Lumpur Regional Centre, ensure that a different (usually more favourable) legal regime is applied for international than for domestic cases.

What matters above everything else is institutional experience, competence and integrity, rather than geographical proximity to one or more of the parties. There are many occasions when it is quite appropriate for (say) Western parties to accept a venue far from home. There are no occasions where any party – no matter where it comes from – should entrust its fate to an unknown institution.

In the following section we provide a brief description of the more important institutions on a regional basis.

(a) Europe

Netherlands Arbitration Institute

The Netherlands provides an arbitration-friendly environment and the Netherlands Arbitration Institute, based in Rotterdam, is an institution of considerable prestige, well adapted to the needs of international arbitration. It has adopted new arbitration rules which came into force on 1 January 1998.

Stockholm Chamber of Commerce

The Stockholm Chamber of Commerce has a long-established reputation in the resolution of East-West disputes (especially between Western European parties and parties from the former Soviet Union or China). Its rules have historically been viewed as more politically acceptable to such countries than those of (say) the ICC. However, this may be changing, given the political changes in Eastern Europe and the creation of an ICC National Committee in China. The Stockholm rules have been substantially revised, with effect from 1 April 1999.

The Stockholm rules are also frequently referred to in the dispute resolution provisions of bilateral investment treaties between Western and Eastern European countries and also feature in the dispute resolution provisions of the Energy Charter Treaty. Under many of these treaties, an investor of one contracting state may commence an arbitration against the other contracting state in the event that the state fails to protect its investment (e.g. by expropriation, failure to honour export quotas and so forth). In those circumstances, the investor often has the option of commencing arbitration under the rules of ICSID, UNCITRAL or the Stockholm Chamber of Commerce: see also Chapter 7 below.

Vienna Arbitral Centre of the Austrian Federal Economic Chamber

The Vienna Centre has carved out for itself a role as a favoured institution in disputes involving Central European parties (in particular Hungary and the Czech Republic).

International Commercial Arbitration Court at the Chamber of Commerce and Industry of the Russian Federation

Although operational since 1932, this institution (ICAC) was reborn in 1993 as a fully functioning international arbitration institution following the modernisation of Russia's international commercial arbitration legislation. Its new rules were promulgated in December 1994. It is worthy of consideration for two main reasons: (a) awards rendered under its rules may, as a matter of practice, be easier to enforce than other arbitration awards against a Russian party within Russia, which is admittedly difficult terrain; and (b) the Court and its President have certain statutory powers which include granting interim measures of protection.

The difficulties of enforcing arbitration awards in Russia and other CIS countries should not be underestimated. However, the involvement of a regional institution such as ICAC may offer a greater prospect of success.

(b) Asia-Pacific

CIETAC

The China International Economic and Trade Arbitration Commission (CIETAC) has supervised and administered international arbitration in China since 1954. The CIETAC Rules were comprehensively revised with effect from 1 October 1995 but have now been replaced by a further revision which came into force on 10 May 1998. However, CIETAC is predominantly a national institution. There have been few cases where both parties were non-Chinese; there have been only a few cases with a non-Chinese presiding arbitrator; and the secretariat of CIETAC is 100% Chinese.

CIETAC handles approximately 800 cases a year. Measured by the number of cases, CIETAC's success is not surprising in that the 1995 Arbitration Law of China effectively gives CIETAC and its maritime equivalent, the China Maritime Arbitration Commission, a monopoly over the conduct of international arbitrations in China. There is also uncertainty as to whether provision can be made for *ad hoc* arbitration or other institutional arbitration under the provisions of the law. A recent government announcement suggested that the domestic arbitration commissions also had jurisdiction to conduct "foreign-related" arbitrations but they are much less well-equipped to do so than CIETAC.

CIETAC's case load is also likely to increase given the recent extension to its jurisdiction to cover disputes arising from *"economic and trade transactions, contractual or noncontractual"*. In the light of the current position, any contract providing for arbitration in China should contain a CIETAC arbitration clause in order to maximise the prospects of enforceability in China. The CIETAC recommended clause is included in Appendix 1.

Hong Kong International Arbitration Centre

The Hong Kong International Arbitration Centre (HKIAC) was formed in 1985 to meet a growing need for arbitration services in South East Asia.

For international arbitration, the HKIAC recommends the use of its Procedure for Arbitration which incorporates the UNCITRAL Arbitration Rules (see above). It does not have its own rules for international arbitration, although it has developed its own set of mediation rules and domestic arbitration rules.

Issues have arisen as to the suitability of using Hong Kong arbitration clauses in relation to awards which may need to be enforced in the PRC following the transfer of sovereignty to the PRC in July 1997, as to which see Chapter 3: Choosing the Place of Arbitration.

Singapore International Arbitration Centre

Following the removal of certain of the restrictions on appearance of foreign counsel in 1992 and in the light of the concerns over the appropriateness of arbitrating China disputes in Hong Kong due in particular to doubts as to the enforceability of Hong Kong awards in China, Singapore has become a much more attractive international arbitration centre. The Singapore International Arbitration Centre (SIAC) was founded in 1990 with the aim of promoting arbitration in

Singapore by offering a modern set of arbitration rules (updated in 1998) and all the necessary support facilities. In its first seven years over 300 cases have been referred to it of which almost 70% are categorised as "international". If current rates of growth in its caseload are maintained, the SIAC is set to become a serious competitor to the Hong Kong International Arbitration Centre, particularly for South and South East Asian arbitrations.

Kuala Lumpur Regional Centre for Arbitration

The Kuala Lumpur Regional Centre was established and is financed by the Malaysian government and aims to provide parties with modern arbitral facilities for arbitrations conducted under the UNCITRAL Rules. Provided the arbitration clause makes clear that the Centre is to be used in conjunction with the UNCITRAL Rules, no judicial intervention is allowed. Otherwise the rather onerous provisions of the domestic arbitration law will apply. Given the lack of flexibility to apply other institutional rules or administer *ad hoc* arbitrations, parties should be cautious before preferring the Kuala Lumpur Regional Centre over other Asian venues such as Hong Kong or Singapore.

(c) The Americas

Inter-American Commercial Arbitration Commission

The Inter-American Commercial Arbitration Commission (IACAC) is an international arbitration institution established in 1934 pursuant to a resolution of the then Conference of American States (now the Organisation of American States) in order to promote an inter-American commercial arbitration system. It is based in Washington DC but operates in co-operation with national sections representing most countries of the Americas.

The role of the IACAC is to resolve, by arbitration or conciliation, international commercial disputes arising in an inter-American context. Although it operates its own set of rules they closely track the UNCITRAL Rules. Its current caseload is limited to about 5 cases per year but it has considerable potential to grow as an institution in the light of increasing trade integration (the target date is 2005 for free trade across the Americas).

There is an additional factor which places the IACAC in a privileged position for the resolution of inter-American commercial disputes. Under Article 3 of the Inter-American Convention on International Commercial Arbitration (the Panama Convention), where nationals of Contracting States have agreed to arbitrate but have not stipulated the procedural regime applicable, the rules of the IACAC will apply in default.

Commercial Arbitration and Mediation Center for the Americas

The Commercial Arbitration and Mediation Center for the Americas (CAMCA) was founded in 1996 as the result of an initiative of the American Arbitration Association, the British Columbia International Commercial Arbitration Centre, the Quebec National and International Commercial Arbitration Centre and the Mexico City National Chamber of Commerce. The initiative arose from Article 2022 of the North American Free Trade Agreement (NAFTA) which specifically requires the Member States (the USA, Canada and Mexico):

> "... to the maximum extent possible, to encourage and facilitate the use of arbitration and other means of alternative dispute resolution for the settlement of international commercial disputes between private parties in the free trade area."

Cases may be filed in the offices of any of the four arbitral institutions listed above and the services of the Centre are available in English, French and Spanish.

CAMCA has its own arbitration and mediation rules which closely track the UNCITRAL Rules and the AAA International Rules but are subject to strict time limits. Recommended clauses are set out in Appendix 4.

Industry-specific institutions

Certain industries, such as the construction, insurance, financial services, shipping and commodities industries have developed their own arbitration and mediation procedures and rules, many of which are long-established.

A more recent example is the rules developed by the World Intellectual Property Organisation (WIPO) for the resolution of intellectual property disputes. In addition to a standard arbitration procedure, the Centre has developed an expedited procedure in response to the particular need in intellectual property disputes for quick results. The expedited procedure provides for a sole arbitrator (rather than a tribunal of three arbitrators), shortened time periods for each of the steps involved in the arbitration proceedings, and abbreviated hearings.

The Centre has also proposed rules providing for emergency relief by arbitrators in response to the need for short term protection of rights in intellectual property disputes, but has encountered conceptual and practical problems, for example over enforceability. The Centre is currently developing rules for the rapid resolution of domain name disputes on the internet via the WIPO Internet Domain Names Process.

Overall, WIPO's small case load reflects a lack of track record and international recognition inevitable in an institution created only in 1994, but the initiatives described above may improve its popularity.

6

Choosing the arbitrators

Arbitration clauses rarely designate arbitrators by name. Indeed, to do so would normally be inadvisable since, by the time the dispute arises, the arbitrators in question may be unable or unwilling to act or may otherwise be unsuitable to determine the particular dispute which has arisen. Yet it is possible to go a long way towards determining the future selection of arbitrators by including appropriate provisions in the contract, a possibility which is often overlooked in the drafting process. At the very least, it is essential to ascertain how the criteria for constituting the arbitral tribunal will be applied if no relevant provision is made in the contract itself.

Number of arbitrators

Many sets of institutional rules, including those of the ICC, the LCIA and the AAA, provide that, if the arbitration clause is silent, the institution will designate a sole arbitrator unless the circumstances justify a three-member tribunal. Nonetheless, in international arbitrations, the preference has traditionally been for three-member tribunals except in cases involving small amounts. For example, in approaching this question, the ICC takes into account the facts in dispute and the likely complexity of the case as well as the amount in dispute. However, presently (1999) a rough rule of thumb used by the ICC is to opt in favour of a three-member tribunal if the amount in dispute is above a range of $1.5–$3.0 million.

CHOOSING THE ARBITRATORS

The LCIA has sometimes specified an arbitral tribunal of three arbitrators regardless of the amount in dispute in order to accommodate the twin objectives of having one arbitrator trained in the applicable law, whilst ensuring that a majority of the members of the tribunal are of a nationality or nationalities different from those of the parties.

It is preferable to resolve the question of the number of arbitrators in the arbitration agreement itself, albeit that parties may consider that this deprives them of a degree of flexibility in responding to the nature and complexity of the dispute. The advantages of referring a dispute to a sole arbitrator are self-evident: meetings and hearings can be arranged more easily and fees and expenses will necessarily be lower than with a three-member panel. The arbitration should also move more quickly, since a sole arbitrator need only make up his or her own mind: he or she will not have to spend time in consultation with colleagues in an endeavour to arrive at a unanimous or majority decision.

There are also disadvantages to the use of a sole arbitrator which should be considered. If the sole arbitrator reaches the wrong decision, there is no Court of Appeal to correct his or her decision. The finality of the arbitration process is, therefore, a good reason to have three arbitrators, except where the cost does not justify it. In addition, given the usual need for a sole arbitrator to be of a neutral nationality, there may not be anyone on the tribunal trained in the law governing the dispute if the governing law is that of the domicile of one of the parties.

In major international contracts, most parties refer disputes to a tribunal of three arbitrators. If the dispute is to be determined by a sole arbitrator and the parties cannot agree who this should be, an arbitrator will be "imposed" upon them by the designated appointing authority or, in the absence of such an authority, by the local court. The arbitrator so chosen may or may not be suitable for the task. What is certain is that he or she will not have been chosen by the parties.

Where the arbitral tribunal consists of three members, these problems are avoided. Each of the parties will usually have the right to nominate one arbitrator, leaving the third arbitrator to be chosen by the two party-nominated arbitrators or in some other agreed manner. (This procedure may not apply in the case of multiple party arbitrations: under the new ICC Rules (Article 10) if there are multiple claimants or respondents who cannot agree on the appointment of a single arbitrator on behalf of all of them, the ICC Court may appoint each member of the arbitral tribunal. Similar provisions exist in the LCIA Rules and AAA Rules.)

The advantage to a party of being able to nominate an arbitrator is that it contributes to a feeling of confidence in the arbitral tribunal. This is particularly important in international arbitrations where, in addition to the matters formally in issue, there may well be differences of legal practice, language, tradition and culture between the parties and, indeed, among the members of the arbitral tribunal themselves. An arbitrator nominated by a party will be able to ensure that that party's case is properly understood by the arbitral tribunal. In particular, any misunderstandings which may arise during the deliberations of the arbitral tribunal (for instance, because of differences of legal practice or of language) can be resolved.

Last but not least, the quality of deliberations of a three-member tribunal should, all things being equal, be greater than that of a sole arbitrator. Even the most able people occasionally make mistakes. When the stakes are high, it may be important to minimise the risk of such mistakes by accepting the extra cost of a three-member arbitral tribunal, particularly as there will generally be no possibility of any review of the merits of the decision.

Parties sometimes express distrust of a three-member arbitral tribunal which contains two party nominees on the ground that the nominees will polarise their positions, with the result that the chair of the tribunal will be forced to split the difference rather than make a clear decision of principle.

Although we concede that there is no reliable research on this question, our own experience has convinced us that such polarisation does not occur as a matter of course (unlike tribunals consisting of partisan arbitrators in certain domestic arbitrations). We do not therefore believe that this constitutes an adequate basis for favouring the choice of a sole arbitrator.

Another perceived disadvantage of three-member tribunals is that one of the party-nominated arbitrators may seek to disrupt the proceedings. Past experience indicates that, very occasionally, a party-nominated arbitrator deliberately obstructs or delays an arbitration in order to create a strategic advantage for the appointing party. This may take many forms including refusal to agree on a third arbitrator or by failing to appear on dates selected for hearings or private deliberations of the arbitral tribunal.

One way of avoiding this type of sabotage – which fortunately seems to be on the wane – is to provide that all three arbitrators will be appointed by the appointing authority. Such a provision, however, defeats the purpose described above of allowing each side to feel that it will have the opportunity to select at least one judge of its choice. This drafting technique therefore seems appropriate only in cases where the perceived need to eliminate party nominations is acute.

A more frequent limitation is that neither side may nominate an arbitrator of its own nationality. Whilst such a provision falls far short of a guarantee of neutrality, it does in practice greatly reduce the potential for partisan arbitrators. Another variation calls upon the administering institution to propose a list of names to each party, giving each side freedom to choose its appointee from that list.

Independence and impartiality of arbitrators

Notwithstanding the common provision for party-nomination in three-member tribunals, it should be remembered that arbitrators in international arbitrations are usually expressly required to be independent and/or impartial. This is contrary to the practice of domestic arbitrations in some jurisdictions where partiality is permitted or even endorsed (e.g. under New York State law). Indeed, arbitrators appointed under the main sets of institutional rules must sign a declaration of impartiality and/or independence before accepting the appointment.

Parties should therefore ensure that, when the time comes, their nominees are not likely to be the cause of delay in the proceedings, for example due to challenges based on a relationship with the parties or their counsel or a financial or other interest in the subject matter of the dispute. Nevertheless, a party-nominated arbitrator may be selected on the basis of a similar political, social, cultural, national or legal background to the selecting party or, for example, through the study of views expressed in writings or lectures.

Appointment in default of agreement or on behalf of a defaulting party

In *ad hoc* arbitration clauses (whether purely *ad hoc* or using the UNCITRAL Rules), the proper formation of the arbitral tribunal either requires agreement between the parties as to the identity of a sole arbitrator or agreement between the parties (or the party-nominated arbitrators) as to the identity of the presiding arbitrator. But what happens if no agreement is reached?

In the case of a pure *ad hoc* clause, it will be necessary to ask the local court in the place of arbitration to appoint the sole or presiding arbitrator. This is unlikely to satisfy either party. First, it will involve national court proceedings before the arbitration has even commenced. Secondly, the choice is likely to be a parochial one with the appointment of a local lawyer not necessarily well versed in the practice of international arbitration or the subject matter of the dispute. In order to avoid criticism of the court appointment process, it is noteworthy that Hong Kong, in the 1996 amendments to its Arbitration Ordinance, now provides for the appointment process to be removed from the courts altogether and given to the Hong Kong International Arbitration Centre. It remains to be seen whether other jurisdictions will follow suit. Outside of Hong Kong, however, the risk of an inappropriate appointment remains a real one.

In order to avoid this risk, parties drafting a pure *ad hoc* clause should provide for an appointing authority which will make the appointment of the sole or presiding arbitrator if the parties cannot agree within a particular time period. Most of the main arbitral institutions are willing to take on this role and will understand the dynamics of the arbitral process and the suitable candidates much better than a national court.

In the case of an *ad hoc* clause adopting the UNCITRAL Rules, the parties are better protected. Whilst it is still important to specify an appointing authority, failure to do so (or failure of the appointing authority to act) enables a party to make a request to the Secretary General of the Permanent Court of Arbitration at The Hague to designate the appointing authority (Article 7 of the UNCITRAL Rules). Parties should note that the Secretary General will not directly appoint the arbitrator (unless the Secretary General is specified as the appointing authority in the contract) but only the appointing authority (usually one of the major arbitral institutions).

How do the main arbitration institutions go about appointing an arbitrator when acting as an appointing authority? When making an appointment on behalf of a defaulting party, some institutions strive to identify an individual who most closely corresponds to the choice the defaulting party is deemed likely to have made if it had not defaulted. This often implies the selection of an arbitrator of the same nationality as the defaulting party. Consideration may be given in appropriate cases to providing that, in the event of default, the appointing authority should choose an arbitrator of a neutral nationality (such as that of the place of arbitration).

CHOOSING THE ARBITRATORS

Selection of sole or presiding arbitrators

Whether or not the arbitration clause calls for party nomination, there remains the problem of choosing the method for selecting the sole or presiding arbitrator – or indeed all the arbitrators in cases where, for example, multiple claimants or respondents are unable to agree on the identity of a party-nominated arbitrator.

Most practitioners prefer to have the appointment made by agreement between the parties or between the arbitrators nominated by them. Some practitioners prefer the former, as it avoids the need for the party-nominated arbitrators to enter into discussions with the lawyers for the party who nominated them to determine the suitability of candidates. It also avoids the risk of the party-nominated arbitrators acting in splendid isolation to agree upon a presiding arbitrator with whom the parties or their lawyers may be uncomfortable for one reason or another. Other practitioners prefer the latter solution because of the central importance to the smooth operation of the proceedings that the presiding arbitrator commands the respect of the other two.

Whichever of the above solutions is adopted, any contractual provisions should provide for a deadline for agreement – at the expiry of which either party may approach the appointing authority to make the appointment.

Qualifications of arbitrators

Whether they are to be nominated by the parties or designated by the appointing authority, arbitrators may be required to have particular qualifications. The most common requirements relate to professional qualifications, language proficiency, nationality and place of residence. Occasionally negative requirements are found, such as the exclusion of arbitrators of the same nationalities as the parties.

It is possible to go too far. The drafter should be careful not to suffocate the clause with too many restrictions, lest no-one remains to fit the bill. Nor should the qualifications be ambiguous or capable of subjective interpretation ('a respected professor of law from ....') in case there may later be room for argument that the composition of the tribunal was not in accordance with the parties' agreement (a ground for challenge under the New York Convention).

We have come across a recent example of a clause which required arbitrators to be senior executives or retired senior executives in a very small specialised branch of a particular industry. The clause called for party nominations and the respondent sought to declare the arbitration agreement void on the basis that there were no arbitrators fitting the description who were ready and willing to act. They were either too busy being senior executives to want to be arbitrators or were conflicted out of the proceedings by their past relationships with one or other of the parties.

Given the danger of being over-specific it is better: (a) to avoid limitations altogether, thereby allowing the maximum flexibility to select the most appropriate person at the time the dispute arises; (b) to impose requirements only if they are fundamental to the efficient operation of the proceedings (for example professional qualifications or language proficiency); or (c), in order to ensure the establishment of an appropriately balanced tribunal, to exclude arbitrators of the same nationality as one of the parties. Whatever requirements are imposed should be stated in objective and unambiguous terms.

Finally, should non-lawyers act as international arbitrators? Under most arbitral rules the parties are free to nominate arbitrators whose field of expertise is not the law. When international institutions appoint international arbitrators, however, they almost invariably select lawyers. This approach is prudent. Whilst an understanding of a range of legal issues, from matters of jurisdiction to private international law, may not be essential in domestic arbitrations, it is generally required in the international context – even in cases which appear at first sight to involve only comparatively simple factual or technical issues.

7

Choosing mechanisms to deal with specific situations

Although many of the circumstances that arise during a dispute cannot be predicted at the time of the contract negotiation, there are several recurring specific situations that the negotiator can anticipate at the drafting stage.

Consolidation and multiparty arbitrations

Certain categories of contracts by definition will involve more than two parties to disputes. This can be seen as problematic, because one of the perceived disadvantages of international arbitration is that it is generally not possible to join additional parties into an existing arbitration without their agreement.

The classic example of a situation where joinder of parties is considered necessary or convenient lies in international construction projects, when the employer enters into a contract with a main contractor, who in turn contracts with various sub-contractors and suppliers. If, for example, the employer has complaints regarding the work done, he must arbitrate against the main contractor, who must then separately seek to recover from the sub-contractor or supplier who may be responsible for the defective work.

In such a situation, it may appear to be desirable for all parties to be brought into the same arbitration proceedings, so as to save time and expense and avoid the risk of inconsistent awards. This approach represents what might be called the broad interests of justice. However, it does not necessarily represent the particular interests of all the parties to a particular dispute, who may not want other parties involved in 'their' arbitration. Taking again the example of the construction contract, the employer does not wish to become involved in a complicated dispute between the main contractor and sub-contractor; but simply looks to the main contractor for compensation, based on the provisions of the main contract alone.

National courts generally have the power to order parties to be joined in court proceedings when it is thought to be necessary or convenient. National laws could also confer such powers of compulsion upon arbitral tribunals. However, to do so would offend against the consensual nature of the arbitral process.

Such an approach it would also lead to difficulties under the present regime for the international enforcement of awards. An arbitral tribunal or an arbitration procedure which is imposed upon parties can hardly be said to be 'in accordance with the agreement of the parties' and recognition or enforcement of an award made in such circumstances may therefore be refused under the New York Convention.

This has not prevented some jurisdictions from enacting legislation providing for the possibility of court consolidation. Thus the courts of Massachusetts, New York, California and the Netherlands all have the power to consolidate arbitral proceedings where common questions of law or fact are involved. Of these jurisdictions, the Netherlands is unique in allowing the parties to contract out of the consolidation provision (Art 1046 of the Netherlands Code of Civil Procedure). The Netherlands Arbitration Institute makes express reference to this right to contract out in its recommended clause in the case of international arbitrations (see Appendix 1).

But court-ordered consolidation of arbitration remains the exception rather than the rule. An alternative approach is to bring about the consolidation of arbitrations in appropriate cases by consent. This can be done via the adoption of arbitration rules providing for consolidation or by separate agreement when an arbitration agreement is being drawn up. The only major international rules to address this point are those of the LCIA (Article 22.1(h)) which provide as follows:

> "22.1   Unless the parties at any time agree otherwise in writing, the Arbitral Tribunal shall have the power...
>
> (h) to allow, only upon the application of a party, one or more third persons to be joined in the arbitration as a party, provided any such third person and the applicant party have consented thereto in writing, and thereafter to make a single final award, or separate awards, in respect of all parties so implicated in the arbitration."

This rule enables the tribunal, upon the application of a single party, to join in one or more third persons who have consented to the joinder in writing. This relaxes the position under the general law whereby *all* existing parties to the arbitration (i.e. including the non-applicant party) would have to be parties to the joinder agreement. However, the provision remains unsatisfactory from the perspective of a main contractor sued by the employer, as the main contractor will want to be sure that the sub-contractor can be brought into the same proceedings whether or not he consents.

Domestic industry arbitration rules have been less circumspect and provide for consolidation at the instance of the institution. The rules of some commodity associations (such as GAFTA) provide for a single arbitration between the first and the last party to the transaction when the dispute arises out of a 'string' contract, with the award binding all contracting parties. The arbitration rules of the US National Association of Securities Dealers also make provision for consolidation at the instance of the institution where separately filed claims are related.

In the absence of any express reference to consolidation in the selected institutional rules, parties should seek to address this predictable issue at the outset and not wait until a dispute has arisen. The idea of an all-embracing decision on any dispute seems more attractive – and is more feasible – at the negotiation stage than when a dispute has arisen and certain parties begin to see the tactical advantage of separate arbitrations.

The most satisfactory solution is to ensure that the parties involved in, say, a major construction project, or in string contracts, execute an arbitration clause in which they specifically agree at the outset to be joined in arbitral proceedings between other parties to a clearly defined series of related contracts. This maintains the essential consensual element required for the arbitral process.

To prevent problems being caused by the subsequent use of a sub-contractor who was not envisaged at the time of executing such an arbitration clause, the main contract should stipulate that the main contractor *must* include the multi-party scheme in any sub-contract, and also provide that his failure to do so would be a breach of the main contract.

Another issue predictably arising out of multiparty arbitrations is the need to balance the number of parties and the equal right of all parties to participate in the constitution of the arbitral tribunal. In the landmark decision of *Siemens* v. *BKMI and Dutco* in 1992, the French Supreme Court upheld a challenge to the jurisdiction of an arbitral tribunal based on the fact that the ICC had required two respondents with diverging interests to nominate an arbitrator jointly, over their objection, whereas the claimant had freely nominated its arbitrator. According to the French court, this breached a rule of international public policy in favour of equality: all parties should be on a level playing field with regard to the constitution of the tribunal. The main institutional rules have been amended to deal with this issue by permitting the institution to appoint the entire tribunal in the event that multiple parties cannot agree on a single nomination: see, for example,

Article 10 of the 1998 ICC Rules and Article 8 of the 1998 LCIA Rules. Although not a perfect solution, this avoids the *Dutco* problem and removes the basis for challenging the international recognition and enforcement of the award.

Much remains to be done before a really successful formula for multiparty arbitration can be achieved, even if it is accepted that this is what parties generally want, before or after a dispute arises. In summary, whilst there was considerable support for it in the 1980s, compulsory consolidation is now recognised as being likely to create more problems that it solves, particularly at the enforcement stage. The ICC's Guide on Multiparty Arbitration, published in 1982, and the subsequent report of its working party on multi-party arbitration, refrained from suggesting model clauses and advised parties to seek specific legal advice. Contract negotiators who contemplate the need to involve more than two parties in a single arbitration should try to cover the position expressly in their arbitration clauses. The appropriate solutions vary greatly according to the circumstances of individual situations, including the law and practice at the place of arbitration.

Adaptation of contracts and filling gaps

In long-term supply agreements or major construction contracts, it is often stipulated that, at stated intervals (or in the event of unexpected supervening events), the parties will renegotiate certain essential terms of the contract.

Such contracts often do not adequately contemplate the consequences of failure of such negotiations. In particular, is it the specific intent of the parties that an arbitral tribunal should have jurisdiction to establish revised terms? In Chapter 2: Choosing the applicable law, we commented that even if the arbitration clause provides for the arbitral tribunal to act as *amiables compositeurs*, this does not necessarily confer upon it the jurisdiction to fill gaps or revise the terms of the contract. If the parties do intend to confer such a power on the arbitral tribunal, they should establish in the contract itself a clear link between the revision clause and the arbitration clause. It should be noted, however, that some arbitration laws, for example the Dutch law and the new Swedish law, specifically provide such authority to arbitrators.

There are a number of techniques for doing so. Their reliability varies according to the contractual context and the applicable law and it is therefore not possible to make recommendations here that would be suitable for general application.

Confidentiality

One of the main reasons cited for choosing arbitration over litigation is that arbitral proceedings are confidential. However, identifying and defining the extent of any obligation of confidentiality in arbitral proceedings has proved to be surprisingly controversial and has resulted in conflicting court decisions within common law jurisdictions, principally in England and Australia.

In a series of cases culminating in the decision of the Court of Appeal in *Ali Shipping* (1998) the English courts have held that there are implied terms concerning confidentiality in each agreement to arbitrate, subject to certain exceptions, for example where disclosure is required in order to enforce the award in subsequent legal proceedings.

By contrast to the approach of the English Courts, the Supreme Court of Victoria in Australia held in a 1995 case, *Esso Australia Resources Ltd*, that confidentiality was not essential to arbitral proceedings and therefore an obligation of confidentiality could not be implied as a matter of law. The parties are, of course, free to agree a provision in an arbitration agreement as to confidentiality but such an obligation should not be implied.

The drafters of legislation and arbitration rules have dealt with the controversy surrounding the duty of confidentiality in differing ways. The English Arbitration Act 1996 does not include any express obligation of confidentiality as it proved to be too difficult and controversial to define. The ICC Rules also do not contain an express provision on confidentiality. By contrast, the LCIA Rules (Article 30) require that all awards, materials produced for the purposes of the arbitration and all other documents produced by another party in the proceedings not otherwise in the public domain should be kept confidential. Similarly, the WIPO Rules contain particularly detailed provisions, reflecting the importance of confidentiality in relation to intellectual property disputes.

As a result, if confidentiality is a special concern to a party, the issue should be specifically addressed at the contract drafting stage: given the difficulty with defining the scope of the obligation of confidentiality and the exceptions to it, any implied term of confidentiality should not be relied upon.

Contracts with state parties

There are a number of issues which arise from a dispute resolution perspective when negotiating contracts with a state or its agencies. First, the commercial party wants to ensure that any arbitration award will be fully enforceable and therefore needs to ensure that the effective waivers of immunity are in place. In addition, the commercial party should consider what (if any) treaty arrangements are in place for the protection of its investment which may provide for the arbitration of disputes directly against the host state of the investment over and above the private contractual arrangements, e.g. bilateral investment treaties (see below).

Waiver of immunity

The only way to place a sovereign party on an equal footing with a private one is to ensure that there is a waiver of immunity from *execution* as well as immunity from *jurisdiction*, the latter being implied by the arbitration clause itself. Such a waiver of execution may be expressed as follows:

> "The [sovereign party] hereby irrevocably waives any claim to immunity in regard to any proceedings to enforce any arbitral award rendered by a tribunal constituted pursuant to this Agreement, including without limitation, immunity from service of process, immunity from jurisdiction of any court, and immunity of any of its property from execution."

This language has been suggested by ICSID. No such clause may, however, be relied upon in all situations. The law of sovereign immunity is complex and varies from one legal system to another. Local and international law advice should be obtained with respect to any contract involving a sovereign party.

Treaty arbitration

In the last few years there has been a plethora of new bilateral investment treaties (BITs) and several multilateral treaties (in particular the North American Free Trade Agreement (NAFTA) and the Energy Charter Treaty) which provide for the arbitration of disputes between private investors and the host state of the investment. The United Kingdom has entered into 69 such treaties and the United States is party to 29. Consequently, if a party is able to demonstrate that the dispute falls within the terms of the relevant treaty, an arbitration may be commenced against the host state. This may provide a helpful safety net, for example if the original contracting party claims force majeure as a result of government intervention. A practical example helps to illustrate the issue:

> A UK company negotiates a contract (containing an arbitration clause) with an Eastern European state oil production association to construct an oil refinery. The UK company is to be paid from the foreign currency

proceeds of refinery products sold by the production association, in respect of which an export quota guarantee has been signed by the host state's Minister of Energy. There is a bilateral investment treaty between the UK and the Eastern European state.

The host government does not honour the export quota guarantee and so the production association has no hard currency funds with which to pay its debt. If the UK company is not paid in accordance with the contract it may commence an arbitration against the production association but the Respondent may well be unable to satisfy an award against it. In those circumstances, the UK company could consider commencing a treaty arbitration directly against the host government under the investment protection provisions of the bilateral investment treaty.

The United Kingdom Model BIT dispute resolution provision (which is fairly typical) provides for a number of alternative arbitration regimes to resolve the dispute:

"Article 8: Settlement of Disputes between an Investor and a Host State

(1) Disputes between a national or company of one Contracting Party and the other Contracting Party concerning an obligation of the latter under this Agreement in relation to an investment of the former which have not been amicably settled shall, after a period of three months from written notification of a claim, be submitted to international arbitration if either party to the dispute so wishes.

(2) Where the dispute is referred to international arbitration, the investor and the [State] concerned in the dispute may agree to refer the dispute either to:
    (a)   the International Centre for the Settlement of Investment Disputes....; or

   (b)   the Court of Arbitration of the International Chamber of Commerce; or

   (c)   an international arbitrator or ad hoc arbitral tribunal to be appointed by a special agreement or established under the Arbitration Rules of [UNCITRAL].

If after a period of three months from written notification of the claim there is no agreement to one of the above alternative procedures, the parties shall be bound to submit it to arbitration under the Arbitration Rules of [UNCITRAL] as then in force."

A similar dispute resolution mechanism exists in the multilateral Energy Charter Treaty which came into effect in April 1998 and which enables any investor of one of the signatory states to commence an arbitration against any host state signatory for breach of the treaty obligations. Three different arbitral regimes are offered: ICSID, UNCITRAL or the Arbitration Institute of the Stockholm Chamber of Commerce.

There is clearly little that can be done at the contract drafting stage to provide for arbitration under BITs or multilateral treaties. Nevertheless, parties should be aware of their existence as part of the underlying dispute resolution protections when transacting with a state and consider providing for arbitration with the contracting party in accordance with one of the same sets of rules available under the Treaty. This would maximise the possibilities of consensual consolidation or, at the very least, the establishment of compatible tribunals.

The need for interim measures

Contract negotiators can accomplish much in relation to the availability of interim measures. Most sets of arbitration rules leave open the possibility of court-ordered provisional remedies such as attachments or injunctions, with the result that the availability of such remedies is a matter of national law. (The ICSID Rules seem to be an exception: Rule 39(5) precludes pre-award court intervention unless the parties have agreed otherwise). Some US courts have been reluctant to grant provisional remedies, on the grounds that to do so would be to interfere with the arbitrator's jurisdiction; the French courts have established a distinction between applications made prior to the designation of the arbitral tribunal (which are freely available) and those made thereafter (which are available only in exceptional circumstances); and numerous other legal systems have not had occasion to pronounce on the subject.

The general trend is that court-ordered provisional remedies are not considered to be inconsistent with an agreement to arbitrate. This is recognised expressly in the ICC, LCIA and UNCITRAL Rules. In cases where it appears particularly important that such remedies should be available it may, however, be advisable to avoid uncertainty and delays by making an express contractual provision to that effect. Such a provision may be drafted as follows:

"By agreeing to arbitration in accordance with this clause, the parties do not intend to deprive any competent court of its jurisdiction to issue a pre-arbitral injunction, pre-arbitral attachment or other order in aid of the arbitration proceedings or the enforcement of any award."

In the 1998 case of *Van Uden*, the European Court of Justice (ECJ) was asked to consider whether or not it was possible to seek interim relief from a court in an EU member state pursuant to Article 24 of the Brussels Convention. This had always been considered to be unavailable since by Article 1(2) the Convention is expressed not to apply to arbitration proceedings.

Van Uden had instituted arbitration proceedings in the Netherlands for breach of contract by Deco Line in refusing to pay a number of invoices. Faced with delays in constituting the tribunal, Van Uden applied to the Dutch courts for interim relief, on the basis of Article 24 of the Convention which deals specifically with provisional and protective measures.

It was held by the ECJ that the existence of an arbitration clause will not exclude an application for interim measures from the scope of the Convention. Such measures are ordered in parallel to arbitration proceedings and subject to establishing a sufficient link between the nature of the interim relief sought and the territorial jurisdiction of the court, interim relief may be awarded notwithstanding that the substantive dispute is subject to arbitration within, or outside, the EU.

It may be even more relevant to specify that the *arbitral tribunal* has authority to make provisional orders. Such authority is in fact already granted under most arbitration rules, but many international arbitrators are hesitant to use it, not wanting to create the impression that they are prejudging the merits. An express provision may help to change this perception and demonstrate that the availability of effective provisional relief – which may be crucial – is part and parcel of the expectations of the parties in agreeing to arbitration.

Such a provision may read as follows:

> "Without prejudice to such provisional remedies in aid of arbitration as may be available under the jurisdiction of a competent court, the arbitral tribunal shall have full authority to grant provisional remedies and to award damages for the failure of a party to respect the arbitral tribunal's orders to that effect."

Getting such provisions incorporated into a contract is easier said than done. At the time of negotiating an agreement, at least one party (such as the employer in a construction contract) may be unwilling to agree in advance to potentially far-reaching measures, such as provisional disposition of property, in the event of a dispute.

And even if such a provision may be accepted, there are many situations in which its practical effect is likely to be disappointing. On the one hand, the prospect of a meaningful provisional order from the arbitral tribunal may be dim due to the urgency with which it must be granted and time that may be taken to establish the arbitral tribunal. On the other hand, the only national court in a position to grant provisional relief may be located in the home country of one of the parties, and unlikely to treat the matter with sufficient neutrality and dispatch.

Attempts during the revision of the main institutional rules to incorporate rules providing for "emergency arbitrators" or "delegates" to make interim measures where the tribunal had not yet been formed have foundered as being impractical, possibly excluding the right of recourse to the courts, and of questionable enforceability under the New York Convention.

'Split' clauses

It is sometimes thought desirable to provide for certain specified disputes or remedies to be referred to arbitration and others to litigation before the courts. In this Guide we have referred to such provisions as 'split' clauses. If such a clause is to be incorporated in a contract, great care should be taken to prevent a preliminary dispute arising between the parties as to the nature of the dispute and, consequently, the procedure to be followed.

The essential point to consider when drafting the clause is for the parties to identify the types of dispute or remedy which they do *not* want to submit to arbitration and then to adopt a suitable form of wording for the purpose. Although the very nature of a split clause makes it difficult to propose a standard form clause of any practical use, the following comments may be of assistance to the drafter:

–   provision may be made for a dispute arising under particular clauses of the relevant contract to be referred to litigation before the courts rather than arbitration.

- alternatively, a general provision may be made for all disputes arising in connection with the relevant agreement to be referred to arbitration whilst
  (1) expressly allowing the parties to seek interim or interlocutory relief from a national court; and/or
  (2) expressly providing for court proceedings to be brought insofar as may be necessary for the enforcement of any arbitral award; and/or
  (3) expressly providing that court proceedings may be brought where the arbitrators have indicated that they are not competent to grant relief of the kind sought and that no other appropriate relief can be granted by them.
- alternatively, the arbitration clause might provide expressly for one party (e.g. the lender in a financial transaction) to have the unilateral right to bring court proceedings in respect of particular types of dispute (e.g. non-payment of an interest instalment). Although not judicially tested, this common type of clause would seem to survive academic criticism that it infringes the principle of mutuality.

Detailed procedural rules

The modern trend, manifested in the best known sets of arbitration rules, is to give arbitral tribunals a wide discretion in matters of procedure (in most cases subject to the agreement of the parties). Depending on the characteristics of the arbitrators, very different approaches may be adopted.

The ICC Rules, like the UNCITRAL Rules, are relatively open-ended. The LCIA Rules are more detailed, but make it clear that most aspects of the rules are not mandatory. In fact, any set of rules which sets out too many mandatory rules of procedure runs the risk of being unpopular in the international arena, as lawyers from different legal cultures may feel that they are not neutral.

Yet it may be an advantage – and certainly it may make life easier for the arbitrators – to make clear from the outset such matters as how witnesses may be heard or the extent to which discovery of documents is to be allowed.

A widely held misconception is that the way in which the evidence will be presented to an arbitral tribunal depends entirely on the place of arbitration. Whilst mandatory rules of the *lex arbitri* (the law governing the arbitration) must be respected in order to avoid any risk of the award being set aside, it is unusual for such law to forbid the parties from agreeing on the way in which evidence is presented to the arbitral tribunal. Modern arbitration proceedings often begin with a discussion between the arbitral tribunal and the parties' representatives as to the procedure to be followed, in particular the way in which evidence is to be presented.

There are essentially four methods of presenting evidence to an arbitral tribunal and these may be categorised as:
– production of contemporaneous documents;
– testimony of witnesses of fact;
– opinions of expert witnesses; and
– inspection of the subject-matter of the dispute.

These methods can be combined in a variety of ways to produce a tailor-made solution for the procedure and presentation of evidence, designed to suit the particular case. It is possible to ensure equality of treatment and due process by imposing some form of agreed structure on the arbitration.

It may still be considered tempting to refer to the rules of procedure of the place of arbitration, but this can be dangerous. Some national arbitration laws leave issues of procedure to the unfettered discretion of the arbitrators, with the result that a reference to local procedural rules may be understood as a reference to the rules of procedure applied by the local national courts. Such rules may not only be inappropriate in the context of an international arbitration, but also unfamiliar to the parties' representatives and indeed to the arbitrators themselves.

The preferred approach is (a) to consider whether the type of disputes that may be anticipated, given the nature of the contract, lend themselves to a particular procedural framework, and (b) to seek to establish an appropriate procedure in the arbitration clause. In many – if not most – instances, no such procedural regime commends itself, and the parties are content to rely on the discretion of the arbitral tribunal. But occasionally the situation is different. For example, joint venture contracts involving a passive partner and a managing partner often provide that the latter is obliged, in the event of any dispute, to disclose operational, technical or financial information.

The UNCITRAL Notes on Organising Arbitral Proceedings, published in 1996, provide a helpful guide through some of the main stages of the arbitral procedure. The Notes provide a list, followed by annotations, of matters which the arbitral tribunal may wish to decide upon, such as the use of institutional rules, the language of the proceedings, place of arbitration, deposits on costs, confidentiality, routing of communications, presentation of evidence etc. The list (without annotations) is reproduced in Appendix 7.

The International Bar Association's Supplementary Rules Governing the Presentation and Reception of Evidence in International Commercial Arbitration (usually referred to as the IBA Rules of Evidence) may also be helpful in establishing a procedure and represent a compromise between common law and civil law approaches. The Rules, which are intended to supplement the chosen rules of arbitration, set out detailed mechanisms for the production of documents; the appearance of witnesses; and the use of expert witnesses (who may be named by the arbitral tribunal or called by the parties). If the Rules are to be adopted, the IBA suggests the following formulation as an addition to the arbitration clause:

"The IBA Rules of Evidence shall apply together with the [ ] Rules governing any submission to arbitration incorporated in this contract. Where they are inconsistent with the aforesaid [ ] Rules, these IBA Rules of Evidence shall prevail but solely as regards the presentation and reception of evidence."

8

Drafting the arbitration clause

In the preceding chapters we have identified the key choices which the contract negotiator must make in deciding upon an effective mechanism for dealing with future disputes. What further considerations need to be addressed in drafting the arbitration clause?

In the absence of special factors, the starting point is that institutional arbitration should be favoured. The most common special factors are where parties are considering a new arbitration agreement for a dispute which has already arisen, or where one of the parties (often a state) is unwilling to submit to institutional arbitration. In such cases, *ad hoc* arbitration under the UNCITRAL Arbitration Rules is recommended.

Where institutional arbitration is contemplated, the choice of institution depends on the many and varied circumstances that may arise in each individual negotiation, such as:
– the nationalities of the parties;
– the nature of the transaction;
– the choice of applicable law and the place of arbitration;
– likely problems in enforceability of the award;
– special regional or other factors.

Non-specialists should not tinker with the model clause recommended by the institution concerned. For example, the deceptively simple language of the ICC model clause ("all disputes arising out of or in connection with the present contract...") covers issues of formation, termination and quasi-contractual tort claims. Attempts at refinement – for

example, "issues regarding the interpretation and performance of this contract" – run the risk of being interpreted as
restrictive and may lead to disputes over the jurisdiction of
the arbitral tribunal.

The use of shorthand can also be a false economy. We represented the claimant in an ICC arbitration in which the abbreviated formulation in an exchange of telexes: *'Arbitration,
if any, by ICC Rules in London'*, was upheld as a valid and
effective clause, but only after years of legal wrangling, as
described in more detail below.

A general purpose model clause

Our recommendation is therefore either to adopt the institution's own model clause intact (see the various examples reproduced in Appendix 1) or to use the following general purpose model clause for institutional arbitration:

> "Any dispute, controversy, or claim arising out of or in
> connection with this contract, including any question
> regarding its existence, validity, or termination, shall
> be finally resolved by arbitration under the Rules of
> [name of institution] in force at [the date hereof/the
> date of the request for arbitration], which Rules are
> deemed to be incorporated by reference into this clause.
>
> The tribunal shall consist of [a sole/three] arbitrator[s].
>
> The place of arbitration shall be [city].
>
> The language of the arbitration shall be [language]."

Checklist for drafting arbitration clauses

Reference to an experienced and reputable institution by
means of the simple model clause proposed above should be
sufficient to create a workable arbitral mechanism. But the

experienced drafter should not be satisfied with that. To eliminate potential pitfalls, the following additional points should be considered:

– *Capacity of the parties to agree to arbitration*

This is a matter for the law of the party whose capacity is in question. For example, may a state or a state entity or a partnership or a private property owner enter into an agreement to arbitrate? In some cases, such questions are sufficiently important for a formal legal opinion to be required, or for a specific contractual warranty to be given.

– *Authority to agree to arbitration*

The authority of representatives is generally a matter of the law of the person or corporate entity being represented. In some legal systems, questions of authorisation are governed by the law of the country in which acts of representation are carried out. The powers of independent agents or brokers should be examined with particular care. A recurrent problem arises in connection with arbitration clauses in corporate by-laws; under some national laws, they are binding only if shareholders expressly accept them at the time of acquiring shares.

– *Applicable substantive law*

The proper law of the contract – whether it is contractually stipulated by the parties or determined afterwards by the arbitral tribunal – also generally determines the validity, scope and effect of the arbitration clause. The parties should therefore consider whether the arbitration clause meets the requirements of the applicable substantive law. If necessary, a different law may be chosen to govern the arbitration clause (e.g. where the award could be challenged in the courts whose domestic law governs the contract, as in the case of Pakistan and previously India: see Chapter 3: Choosing the Place of Arbitration).

DRAFTING THE ARBITRATION CLAUSE

– *Procedural law*

The modern consensus is that arbitrations should be conducted in accordance with the mandatory rules of the law of the place of arbitration. This need not be spelled out in the arbitration clause. Occasionally it may be acceptable to stipulate that the procedural law shall be that of the place of arbitration, including non-mandatory rules. Such a provision should, however, not be accepted without the benefit of expert local advice. Provisions to the effect that the arbitration should be conducted in accordance with the law of a country other than the place of arbitration are potentially dangerous (because they increase the risk of post-arbitration litigation in national courts) and should usually be avoided.

– *Arbitrability of disputes under the law applicable to the arbitration clause or, if different, the place of arbitration or the likely place of enforcement*

If the dispute is not arbitrable, any resulting award is likely to be unenforceable. The most frequent problems arise in relation to disputes that involve competition, bankruptcy and intellectual property law, as well as employment and distribution agreements. For example, a contract drafter in Europe should know that although an arbitral tribunal may initially decide issues of European competition law, if the matter is pressed to the end the final authority is necessarily the European Court of Justice. Likewise, issues as to the validity of an entry on a public register (e.g. a registered patent or trade mark) will be for the appropriate national courts to determine.

– *Exclusion of appeals on the merits*

The ICC and LCIA Rules both contain provisions to the effect that, by agreeing to arbitration thereunder, the parties waive all recourse or rights of appeal insofar as such waiver is legally permissible. Parties who want finality must ensure that the rules to which they refer (or the arbitration clause itself) contain a similar provision. For example, the UNCITRAL

Rules do not contain an express provision and appropriate language should be included in the clause (see Appendix 1).

This crucial feature must, however, be examined in light of the legal position at the place of arbitration. The provision in the ICC and LCIA Rules has been held to be effective as a matter of English law to exclude appeals to the court on the merits. In Switzerland, on the other hand, it is generally accepted that the possibility of *total* exclusion of any recourse to the Swiss courts (including challenges on the grounds of excess of authority or violation of the right to be heard) requires an express provision in the arbitration clause. (Since the general rule in Switzerland is that awards may not be challenged on the merits, the desirability of such a *total* exclusion is in any event questionable). Generally, it is considered that contractual exclusion clauses cannot remove all possible recourse to the courts in most jurisdictions, as some limited recourse is mandatory.

Some occasionally significant elements

Chapter 7 – "Choosing mechanisms to deal with specific situations" comments on, *inter alia:*
– consolidation and multiparty arbitration;
– adapting contracts and filling gaps;
– waiver of immunity by state parties; and
– split clauses.

Chapter 9 is devoted to intermediate dispute resolution and ADR clauses. The experienced international drafter should consider such mechanisms as a matter of routine.

The following points may also be significant:

Method of selection and qualifications of the arbitrators

Although all the sets of arbitration rules considered in this Guide deal with these issues, the parties are generally free to vary them (see Chapter 6 – "Choosing the arbitrators").

Costs

The power of the arbitral tribunal to award costs in an international arbitration arises from a combination of the agreement of the parties, the law governing the arbitration agreement, the law of the place of arbitration and the law of the place where recognition or enforcement of the award may be sought. The Rules of the ICC, LCIA, UNCITRAL and the AAA all allow arbitral tribunals a wide discretion to award costs, including the fees of the parties' lawyers.

Nevertheless, it is still important to consider the way in which arbitral tribunals in a particular country are likely to exercise their discretion, since this varies from place to place. This should be taken into consideration when choosing the arbitrators as their differing attitudes (dependent upon their nationality and legal background) are likely to influence how they exercise their discretion (e.g. the English tradition is to award the costs of legal representation to the successful party up to a "reasonable" level; the American tradition is to award little or nothing).

Occasionally, parties wish to include an express provision in the arbitration clause to the effect that full costs shall be awarded to the successful party (on the theory that this may inhibit the presentation of speculative claims) or, to the contrary, that each side shall bear its own costs (on the assumption that any dispute will be a gentleman's disagreement and that in the interest of future relations insult should not be added to injury). Although in England Section 61 of the Arbitration Act 1996 gives the arbitral tribunal a discretion to award costs, Section 60 provides that any provision in an agreement for the arbitration of *future* disputes that a party or the parties shall in any event pay their own costs, is void. (It has also been suggested that this is because such a provision might be inserted deliberately in standard form terms of business to deter consumers from making claims against a large and powerful organisation). It is difficult therefore to specify any general practice as to the treatment of costs in international arbitrations.

Incorporation by reference

Arbitration is possible without including an arbitration clause in the contract. An agreement may be reached that a transaction will be subject to the general conditions of a particular industry or corporation. Such an approach obviously saves time and enables parties to adhere to a complex contract by a rapid exchange of faxes or other forms of communication. And if such general conditions include an arbitration clause, their acceptance may well be effective to create arbitral jurisdiction. Some precautions are nevertheless required.

First, this approach makes it necessary to check not only the clarity of the reference to the general conditions, but also the sufficiency of the arbitration clause contained in those conditions. Some arbitration clauses found in the small print of general conditions appear to have been designed for another age.

Secondly, the courts of many countries are suspicious of an incorporation-by-reference mechanism. They wonder (often rightly) whether in agreeing the general conditions the parties gave any thought to the fact that they were submitting to arbitration, particularly if it is arbitration abroad. As a result, national courts are more likely to decline to give effect to such an arbitration clause than when they are confronted by a clause adopted by an express provision in the contract.

In a consumer or employment context, it may be that arbitration clauses which select a place of arbitration will deprive a weak party of basic procedural safeguards. Forum selection clauses will not be given effect by the US courts in consumer or employment cases unless the clause has been agreed after the dispute has arisen or if it grants the consumer/employee a right to sue or be sued at his/her place of domicile. Similar protection for consumers and employees is provided by the provisions of the Brussels and Lugano Conventions.

We therefore recommend that, even if parties seek to create an instant contract by referring to pre-existing general conditions, they should if possible make an explicit reference to the arbitration provisions in those conditions. The results need not be cumbersome, as in the following hypothetical example:

> "We agree to deliver FOB your vessel at Trondheim between 5 and 15 September 1999 5000 tonnes grade 3 quality pulp. Current General Conditions of Scandinavian Pulp Exporters Association to apply. Arbitration under Rules of Stockholm Chamber of Commerce Institute, as per Clause 14 said General Conditions. Please notify your acceptance by return."

A common problem for parties using this approach – which is intended to be lightning-quick and therefore informal – is that senders and recipients of such messages seldom check whether their counterparts have requisite authority to bind the entity they represent: see above.

Pitfalls

– Any assumptions about the authority of purported representatives, the capacity of any party to bind itself to arbitration (especially if it is a state entity), or the arbitrability of foreseeable disputes are made at your peril.

– Do not equivocate. If the parties want arbitration to be an exclusive remedy, they must make that clear. If they want arbitration as an *available* remedy, although not necessarily exclusive, they should make clear that if one of them opts for arbitration, the other may not neutralise the proceedings by going to court. In practice, there are a surprising number of instances of non-choice, through the adoption of pathological clauses like the following:

> "In case of arbitration, the _____ Rules of Arbitration shall apply; in case of litigation, any dispute shall be brought before the courts of _____".

Such a provision leads to confusion, waste and frustration.

– Do not designate an appointing authority without first verifying its willingness to accept that responsibility. Parties have found to their regret that judges in a neutral country have declined to become involved in a dispute between foreigners, with the result that the arbitration agreement becomes inoperable and the claimant is left with the prospect of litigating before national courts in what may be hostile territory.

– Do not attempt to combine irreconcilable procedural laws. Quite often, negotiators reach unfortunate compromises, such as accepting a venue in country X in return for application of the procedural law of country Y. If the law of country X contains mandatory provisions with respect to any arbitrations taking place within that country, and those are inconsistent with the laws of country Y, intractable problems may arise.

– Do not accept a reference to rules or institutions unless you are certain that they exist and that they are acceptable. It is surprising how often contracts refer to non-existing institutions, or to institutions that have no arbitration rules, or to a known institution but using an incorrect appellation.

– Do not try to improve on the model clauses of arbitral institutions unless you are sure of what you are doing. There is always the risk that if model clauses are amended, the institution will refuse to administer the arbitration.

– Do not use shorthand if this results in any ambiguity which might be exploited by a recalcitrant defendant. In one case, we represented a Kazakhstan oil producer in a dispute over payment for a shipment of crude oil to an American trading corporation. The contract was concluded by means of an exchange of telexes and included a provision for English law, together with an abbreviated formulation for the arbitration clause, which read: *'Arbitration, if any, by ICC Rules in London'.*

ICC arbitration proceedings were duly commenced when the American defendant failed to pay. The American defendant duly objected to the jurisdiction of the ICC arbitrators, which objection failed, and then threatened to challenge the validity of the clause in a 'court of competent jurisdiction'. A US jury trial loomed large! We applied instead to the English court for a declaration that the clause was valid. Nearly a year's worth of proceedings before the English court followed, with the defendant claiming rectification of the contract and/or that the clause merely provided that *if* the parties later agreed to arbitrate rather than litigate any disputes, they would use the ICC Rules for an arbitration in London. During all this time the arbitration proceedings were suspended.

Eventually the English court delivered its verdict affirming that the clause constituted a valid, effective and binding agreement to arbitrate. However, in the time taken for the court to rule on that question, the defendant had ample opportunity to delay the prosecution of the claim against it in the arbitration, and to protect its assets from execution. (The defendant refused to participate substantively in the arbitration and an award was duly rendered against it).

If the roles were reversed, the Kazakhstan party would be vilified as someone who refused to play by the rules of the international game which it had recently been allowed to join. But a root cause of the problem was in the way the clause was drafted. The shorthand formula no doubt seemed appropriate and effective at the time. But much agony could have been avoided with more careful drafting, for example by following the ICC's recommended language: see Appendix 1.

Ad hoc arbitration clauses: caveat draftsman

The problem with *ad hoc* clauses is not merely that it is important to consider the questions mentioned above. It is also often necessary to draft express provisions to cater for them. This arises particularly in the context of the consequences of default. Free-standing *ad hoc* clauses are typically several pages long (see Appendix 2 for an example): and even when reference is made to established rules, there is no institutional back-up to perform such administrative acts as appointing arbitrators or extending time limits for awards – failing which, cumbersome applications to the courts must be made or in some legal systems, the arbitration will be a nullity.

9

Intermediate dispute resolution and ADR

In modern usage the term 'alternative dispute resolution', or ADR, originated in the USA. Its popularity there – and its increasing support in other jurisdictions – reflects a high degree of frustration with the cost, delays and trauma often associated with traditional dispute resolution procedures. ADR is now widely used in many countries, partly through the establishment of organisations dedicated to the promotion and use of ADR and increasingly through court-mandated schemes.

The expression ADR is sometimes taken to include arbitration. This causes confusion. Whilst arbitration is undoubtedly an alternative to recourse to national courts, it is nevertheless intended to lead to a binding and enforceable determination of a dispute. In this sense it should be contrasted with the many forms of ADR which involve a consensual (rather than adjudicative) process, often with the involvement of a neutral third party.

The option of using ADR procedures may be considered either at the contract drafting stage, by inserting an ADR clause in the contract itself, or after a dispute has already arisen. One advantage of the former approach (for example, by providing for a mandatory 'cooling off' period before either party commences arbitration or other proceedings) is that invoking the agreed procedure need not appear to be a sign of weakness. However, ADR should *not* be seen as an 'alternative' in the sense of being a substitute for the adjudicatory process. The contract must contain an effective mechanism for referring the dispute to arbitration or to litigation in the courts, in case the consensual approach proves unsuccessful, within a prescribed period of time.

Principal forms of ADR

There are many variations on the types of ADR described below. One of the values of the process is that it may be precisely tailored in each case to suit the parties' specific requirements.

The most widely-known forms of ADR are mediation, conciliation, mini-trial, non-binding arbitration, expert opinion and early neutral evaluation. Most forms of ADR share the same essential features. The process is intended to encourage representatives of the parties to recognise the weaknesses of their own case and the strengths of their opponent's case, as well as the wider commercial implications of the dispute. By negotiating face-to-face, concessions can be made and opportunities for compromise explored without prejudicing the parties' legal rights, at least until some form of binding agreement is reached. But it is the role of the third party – someone who is independent of the parties and able to view the dispute objectively – which is usually the crucial element. The success of any particular ADR process will largely depend upon that individual's skills in bringing the parties together and finding areas of agreement.

The terms "conciliation" and "mediation" are not terms of art. They are frequently used interchangeably, and there is no generally accepted or consistent usage. Hence, the definitions offered below are not by any means universally agreed. Some take the view that the conciliator merely "shuttles" between the parties, in an attempt to "facilitate" settlement without making his or her own recommendations, whilst the mediator will usually draw up and propose terms of settlement. Others, with equal conviction, take the opposite view. It should also be noted that the process may, as it develops, move from one form to the other.

Negotiation

Contractually mandated "good faith" negotiations between the parties may be viewed as a form of ADR. A clause to that effect will usually provide for a "cooling off" period and prevent recourse to arbitration (or litigation) before a certain time period has elapsed. It may be effective in focusing the parties' minds on the advantages of settlement at the initial stages of the dispute rather than on the tactical advantages to be gained by the commencement of proceedings. It must, however, be subject to a time limit to prevent a recalcitrant party from arguing that arbitration cannot be commenced because negotiations are continuing. Common time periods are 30 or 60 days. It is questionable whether the triggering of a contractual negotiation period will stop time running for limitation purposes, without express agreement to that effect.

Mediation

An impartial third party employed by the parties to act as a mediator does not usually make recommendations or render decisions. Rather, he or she assists the parties to negotiate their own solution to the dispute. The parties can agree on whether or not the mediator is to consult with them separately (known as "caucusing"), jointly or both. A mediator cannot compel the parties to reach a settlement, though he or she may take a very actively persuasive approach.

Conciliation

A conciliator is also appointed by agreement between the parties but will usually take a more active role in the negotiations than a mediator and may well make recommendations as to what he or she would regard as a fair resolution of the dispute. In order to establish the parties' respective negotiating positions, the conciliator should be allowed to see the parties privately. However, as in the case of the mediator, a conciliator cannot compel the parties to reach a settlement and has no power to impose a binding "award" on the parties.

Mini-trial/executive tribunal

The parties' legal representatives present their respective cases (in abbreviated form) to a panel, usually consisting of a senior executive from each party with a neutral chairman (often a retired judge or other senior lawyer) presiding. The chairman of the panel may simply ensure fair play, or may intervene to help the parties to resolve the problem. If the latter approach is adopted, the process is sometimes referred to as 'moderation'.

Although the term "trial" is a misnomer, this process does, as the name suggests, involve a more detailed examination of the strengths and weaknesses of the parties' respective legal positions. It is also likely to result in a non-binding decision which the parties may use as the basis of, or a factor in, further settlement negotiations. Whilst it is tempting to recommend use of the process at the earliest possible stage (so as to maximise savings of costs), it is unlikely to be effective until after at least an initial exchange of pleadings and disclosure of documents.

Non-binding arbitration

The process is sometimes referred to as 'trial-run' arbitration or adjudication. An arbitrator appointed by the parties may make a finding on a particular aspect of the case, or make a reasoned award based on a limited review of documents submitted by the parties and other evidence. His or her decision is not binding but the parties may subsequently agree to accept it.

Expert opinion or fact-finding

The parties may at any stage of a dispute seek the opinion of an independent expert (such as a specialist in a given technical field) on one or more aspects of the case. The parties are not bound by the opinion but may subsequently agree to accept it.

The ICC's International Centre for Technical Expertise provides a mechanism for such expert evaluation. The Centre's model clause is reproduced in Appendix 3.

Early neutral evaluation

As an extension of the use of experts on technical issues it may be desirable to obtain an independent evaluation of the parties' respective cases – legal issues as well as factual or technical matters – in relation to anticipated or actual legal proceedings. This may be done *ad hoc* or by involving one of the ADR organisations referred to below. One example is the City Disputes Panel's procedure for obtaining a non-binding, reasoned evaluation of the case by an authoritative panel, without prejudice to the parties' legal claims and defences. Such an evaluation may encourage settlement and prevent unnecessary proceedings, saving both time and money.

ADR organisations

In recent years a number of organisations have been established specifically to promote and encourage the use of ADR. Of these the Center for Public Resources in the USA is still the most important and well-established. JAMSEndispute is also very active in the USA. In the UK, the Centre for Dispute

Resolution has, since its establishment in 1990, made a significant contribution to the awareness of ADR, as have the City Disputes Panel, formed in April 1994 and aimed principally at resolving disputes in the financial services sector, and the Academy of Experts.

The CPR Institute for Dispute Resolution

Of the organisations dealing exclusively with ADR, the CPR Institute for Dispute Resolution (CPR) is recognised as the leading authority in the USA. It is a non-profit making body dedicated to the promotion of ADR and has a wide-ranging membership throughout the legal and business community. CPR compiles a register of subscriber companies, who have adopted the CPR corporate policy statement of the "pledge" advocating the use of ADR as an alternative to litigation. The text includes the following:

> "In the event of a business dispute between our company and another company which has made or will then make a similar statement, we are prepared to explore with that other party resolution of a dispute through negotiation or ADR techniques before pursuing a full-scale litigation. If either party believes that a dispute is not suitable for ADR techniques, or if such techniques do not produce results satisfactory to the dispute, either party may proceed with litigation."

CPR publishes details of neutrals who are qualified to act in ADR disputes, as well as specialist panels who act in certain regions, or in relation to certain types of dispute. CPR also offers training programmes aimed at improving knowledge of and proficiency in ADR procedures, and produces a regular newsletter, practice guides and other publications. CPR has formulated rules and model procedures, including some which are specifically tailored to certain types of dispute.

An example from a series of mediation clauses recommended by CPR is reproduced in Appendix 3.

The Centre for Dispute Resolution

The Centre for Dispute Resolution (CEDR) is also an independent non-profit making organisation which aims to promote and encourage the use of ADR in the UK. Since its launch in November 1990 it has gained widespread support and its membership includes business, industrial and professional organisations throughout the country.

CEDR offers a wide variety of services to members, including training, access to accredited neutrals, guidance on model ADR clauses in contracts, rules and procedures for resolving disputes, seminars and training on negotiation and different ADR techniques, and newsletters covering recent developments.

In June 1991, CEDR entered into a joint collaboration agreement with the LCIA, whereby parties are offered the reciprocal services of both organisations. Disputes may be submitted initially to ADR under the auspices of CEDR, and if unsuccessful are referred to arbitration under the LCIA Rules.

Two model mediation clauses recommended by CEDR are reproduced in Appendix 3.

The City Disputes Panel

The City of London-sponsored City Disputes Panel (CDP) also offers a wide variety of dispute resolution services, particularly for use in disputes in the financial services sector, ranging from arbitration, mediation and conciliation to neutral non-binding case evaluation. The CDP maintains lists of experienced judicial and industry figures who may be selected to resolve disputes according to the nature of the issues involved.

Model mediation and other clauses recommended by The City Disputes Panel are reproduced in Appendix 3.

ADR procedures

Institutions such as the ICC, the AAA, ICSID and UNCITRAL have established conciliation rules which may be adopted by the parties in their contracts. Specialist ADR bodies such as CEDR and the City Disputes Panel have developed their own mediation and other rules and procedures. Examples of model clauses recommended by such organisations are reproduced in Appendix 3. Alternatively, the parties may design their own *ad hoc* procedure (see also Appendix 3).

Intermediate dispute resolution

It is increasingly common, especially in contracts involving long term projects or commercial relationships, for parties to agree upon varying forms of staged or intermediate dispute resolution procedures, such as expert adjudications or decisions by review boards, which must be followed prior to the commencement of arbitration proceedings. Such clauses are most often seen in contracts for construction or infrastructure projects, where numerous disputes may be anticipated during the life of the contract which, except in a few cases, need to be resolved quickly and expeditiously without recourse to full-blown arbitration proceedings.

Concern had been raised that the use of intermediate dispute resolution procedures might not (unlike arbitration) require the courts to stay (suspend) judicial proceedings, thereby allowing parties to commence proceedings in national courts prematurely. As far as the English courts are concerned these concerns were allayed in the *Channel Tunnel* case where it was held that the English court had an inherent power to stay proceedings before it whilst the chosen dispute resolution procedure was followed. This has now been enshrined in section 9(2) of the English Arbitration Act which states:

> "An application [to stay court proceedings in favour of arbitration] may be made notwithstanding that the matter is to be referred to arbitration only after exhaustion of other dispute resolution procedures"

Intermediate dispute resolution is not new in the context of major projects. Clause 67 of the 1987 FIDIC conditions of contract for use in major international construction projects provides for disputes to be referred first to the designated Engineer and then to arbitration under the ICC Rules if the Engineer's decision is not accepted by either party. Claims arising in the course of the project (for example, claims by the contractor for the cost consequences of unforeseen working conditions) may be dealt with (and, if appropriate, interim payments made) in a manner which requires the contractor to continue working, notwithstanding that other disputes may be unresolved. In this way, disputes may be resolved at an early stage in an informed manner by a person with a working knowledge of the project.

In practice, the contractor may take a cynical view of the Engineer's decision as he is usually on the payroll of the Employer and is often asked to review his own decisions. In order to meet this criticism, contracts for major projects often include provisions for disputes to be referred first to a standing panel of independent experts and FIDIC has recently made provision for such panels.

The Engineer's or Panel's decision provides a filtering procedure whereby some, if not necessarily all, disputes can be resolved quickly and expeditiously, thus maintaining a degree of co-operation between the parties. It can, however, also be seen as merely an additional step in the procedure, each party knowing that decisions by the Engineer or Panel may subsequently be reviewed in arbitration, if either party so requires.

Versions of this multi-layered approach were adopted not only in the Eurotunnel contract but also in other major infrastructure projects such as the Hong Kong Airport Core Programme and the Boston Central Artery/Tunnel Project. The nature of this Guide does not permit a detailed analysis of these mechanisms but a brief review of the techniques used may assist contract drafters when considering suitable mechanisms in the context of major projects.

Eurotunnel

Under the dispute resolution provisions of the Eurotunnel contract, a standing panel of five experts was appointed which ensured ready access to a range of technical expertise and experience. Each party had the right to nominate two engineers and a legally qualified chairman was subsequently agreed. The panel was given regular reports as to the progress of the project which, coupled with its ongoing exposure to disputes, ensured an increasing level of familiarity.

Any dispute would be referred first to a panel of three members consisting of the chairman and one each of the party-nominated engineers who were obliged to render a decision in writing within 90 days. If either party were dissatisfied with a decision of the panel then within 90 days of receiving notice of the panel decision they would have to refer the matter to arbitration under the rules of the ICC with a seat in Brussels. In the meantime, the contractors had to continue work on the project and abide by any decision of the panel.

The benefit of such a two-stage process is obvious: it filters claims to ensure that only the most contentious matters end up in full scale arbitration, thereby ensuring that the project is not continuously dogged by legal proceedings. To that extent it was a success. Only four disputes resulted in arbitration and two were settled prior to the award.

The Boston Central Artery/Tunnel Project

This project is one of the most complex highway projects ever undertaken, with a cost in excess of US$6 billion. The dispute resolution provisions in the contracts consist of four filters prior to arbitration. The first stage (which is preventive) is "partnering" which consists of an educational programme aimed at ensuring each of the participants understands and works towards achieving the common goal. The first "post dispute" stage is the presentation of a dispute to an authorised representative who, in his capacity as an expert, investigates and decides upon the claim. If the parties are not satisfied with the decision of the authorised representative they may refer the matter to a "Dispute Review Board" (DRB) consisting of two technical experts and a chairperson qualified in the field of dispute resolution. The DRB is established at the outset of the relevant contract. The proceedings before the DRB involve the submission of written briefs attaching relevant documents but there is no formal hearing. At any stage in the DRB proceedings prior to the issuance of a decision the parties may refer the matter to mediation or other form of ADR. Over 90% of disputes which have arisen under the project have been resolved through this filtering system.

Hong Kong Airport Core Programme

The dispute resolution mechanism employed for the Hong Kong Government's contracts for the construction of the new Hong Kong airport consists of four stages:
(a) engineer's decision;
(b) mediation;
(c) adjudication;
(d) arbitration.

The mediation process, which is a prerequisite to formal adjudication, may be invoked at any time and is administered by the Hong Kong International Arbitration Centre. The adjudication process provides for a formal exchange of pleadings and the right to call witnesses and commission expert evidence, subject to a time delay of 42 days for the adjudicator to render his reasoned decision in writing. If either of the parties is unhappy with the decision of the adjudicator, they may commence arbitration proceedings by service of a Notice of Arbitration under an *ad hoc* arbitration procedure with the Hong Kong International Arbitration Centre acting as the appointing authority.

Advantages and disadvantages of ADR

For all the wealth of commentary about the theory of ADR there is still comparatively little information publicly available about how ADR has worked in practice, what particular problems have been encountered and how they have been addressed. Nevertheless, it is possible to make certain general observations about the advantages and disadvantages of the process as a whole.

Flexibility

ADR offers great flexibility in that the parties are free to choose the most appropriate method of dispute resolution and the procedure to be used. In addition, the parties are free to adopt an unlimited range of solutions, and are not simply restricted to a cash award, so that the chance of reaching a mutually acceptable compromise is enhanced.

Focusing on the main issues

The involvement in the ADR process of a neutral expert individual or panel tends to focus the proceedings more clearly, and avoids the risk of encountering a judge or jury who may be unfamiliar with the technical issues frequently involved in commercial disputes. In addition, all parties should be free to focus on the facts and not be diverted by procedural issues.

The intervention of a neutral third party may also assist the parties in separating themselves and their emotions from the problem and encourage them to concentrate their energies more intensively on the real issues. Senior management are also forced to adopt a more 'hands on' approach, instead of transferring the initiative to their lawyers.

Speed

Disputes can be resolved by certain types of ADR procedures in a matter of days or weeks, as opposed to the months and years often involved in litigation or arbitration.

Apart from the obvious costs savings, the speedy resolution of disputes minimises the drain on management time and associated corporate disruption and also limits the risk of adverse publicity.

Cost

As a quicker and simpler method of dispute resolution, ADR is usually considerably cheaper than either arbitration or litigation.

It is also worth noting that, even if ADR proves unsuccessful, the parties will often have resolved a subset of issues and gone some way towards preparing themselves for any subsequent proceedings.

Success rate

Reportedly, 80–90% of cases which go to ADR are successfully resolved. Furthermore, a significant number of cases which do not settle during the ADR process nevertheless settle very shortly after the end of the formal process, quite possibly as a result of the impetus and movement in positions gained from that process.

Confidentiality

Unlike litigation in the courts, ADR proceedings are carried out in private. This avoids the possibility of adverse publicity, and can also minimise the risk of disclosing business information and trade secrets to competitors.

On-going business relationship

ADR provides an effective means of resolving disputes between parties who have an interest in maintaining an ongoing business relationship. The parties approach the process in a spirit of negotiation and compromise, instead of adopting the adversarial positions associated with litigation and arbitration. They are encouraged to focus on business objectives rather than legal wrangles. Both parties are given the chance to air their views and, ideally, due to the flexible nature of the settlement reached, neither party will feel that it has 'won' or 'lost' its case, but both will come out of the process with a measure of satisfaction.

Examples

Texaco/Borden case

An often-quoted example of the 'win-win' results of ADR is that of the US$200 million anti-trust suit between Texaco and Borden in the USA arising out of a gas supply contract. Proceedings were filed in May 1980. After years of interlocutory battles and massive discovery, shortly before a preliminary trial date the two corporations agreed to resolve their differences by mini-trial. After a final exchange of information in writing and a short oral presentation to executive vice-presidents appointed to the panel by each company, the dispute was resolved and the parties entered into a major new gas supply contract worth many millions of dollars. The whole process is said to have taken less than three weeks.

British & Commonwealth Holdings/Atlantic Computers case

A more recent example demonstrating some of the advantages of ADR is the successful mediation between British & Commonwealth Holdings (B&C) and Atlantic Computers. The litigation between B&C and Atlantic concerned a claim brought by B&C of more than £850m, related to B&C's acquisition of Atlantic Computers in 1988 and the subsequent collapse of both companies in 1990. The proceedings commenced in 1994. A trial had been fixed for May 2000 and was expected to last between 12 and 15 months. Following the biggest-ever European mediation conducted with the support and approval of CEDR, the litigation was settled in January 1999. At least two years of time were saved as a result along with the attendant high costs involved in litigating to trial.

UK Government/Arthur Andersen case

A further example is the settlement between the UK Government and Arthur Andersen, after 12 years of litigation arising out of the De Lorean collapse and following an order made by the English Commercial Court encouraging the parties to attempt ADR. Both parties protested (unsuccessfully) against the imposition of the order, and yet went on to reach a settlement.

ADR is not appropriate in all cases

- Both parties must have a genuine interest in settlement. ADR is unlikely to be effective if there is a great deal of antipathy or animosity between the parties, or where an action is being instituted or defended for tactical reasons. Similarly, it is unlikely to be successful in cases where delay is beneficial to one of the parties, or where there is a large discrepancy in the parties' wealth and resources and, consequently, their bargaining position.

- ADR is not appropriate where it is necessary to create a binding and public precedent, for example where a significant issue of law is involved, or where the dispute involves the interpretation of a clause in a widely-used standard form contract. However it is theoretically possible to obtain rulings on legal issues through traditional means, and revert to ADR for factual findings and an eventual settlement. (The process of adjudication or expert opinion might also be used in this way.)

- Some parties express concern that suggesting ADR may be taken by their opponent as a sign of weakness. This attitude is, however, far less prevalent than it was a few years ago. Indeed, in main-stream litigation in the English High Court, parties must confirm that there has been a genuine consideration of ADR before they are permitted to proceed to trial. In any event any fears of appearing weak may be allayed by incorporating an ADR clause into the contract initially, or perhaps by a corporation associating itself with ADR organisations or issuing a general policy statement supporting the use of ADR, such as CPR's 'pledge'.

- Whilst most ADR procedural rules provide that admissions or concessions made by a party during the ADR process cannot be used against that party in any subsequent proceedings, there may be a residual concern about revealing one's hand in case the process later breaks down.

– Finally, it is sometimes argued that ADR attempts to formalise negotiation methods that have long existed on an informal footing, and therefore has the effect of *reducing* the available avenues for compromise. This will, however, largely depend upon the attitudes and abilities of both the parties and the neutral third party.

Checklist for drafting ADR clauses

The exercise of drafting a 'model' ADR clause illustrates the nature of the ADR process, namely that it depends for its success largely upon the willing co-operation of the parties (although the Government/Arthur Andersen case suggests this is not necessarily, at least initially, a vital element). Provisions *requiring* parties to resolve disputes amicably – with or without the intervention of a third party – are inevitably hollow-sounding. An ADR clause may not be able to compel a party to approach the resolution of a dispute with an open mind, but a structure can be devised within which – given a spirit of co-operation between the parties – a solution can be found which is acceptable to all concerned.

The clause may refer to various matters (for example, procedural aspects) which are to be agreed by the parties – or determined by the third party – after the dispute has arisen. The clause itself must provide a framework within which either party may invoke the ADR process without such a step appearing as a sign of weakness or lack of confidence in its strict legal position and, most importantly of all, must contain an effective mechanism for referring the dispute to arbitration or some other formal means of resolution if the ADR process breaks down within a prescribed period of time.

Circumstances will vary according to the nature of the transaction and the range of likely disputes, but the following particular matters usually should be taken into consideration:

– Should there be a provision for face-to-face negotiations between the parties before involving a neutral adviser?

- When is the ADR procedure deemed to commence?

- What is the effect of the ADR procedure on any ongoing proceedings? Will they be stayed? If so, how and when can they be re-started in the event that the ADR procedure breaks down?

- What mechanism should be used for agreeing/appointing a neutral adviser?

- Should the neutral adviser's qualifications be agreed in advance?

- Should the clause provide for an outside agency (e.g. CPR or CEDR) to be involved in appointing a neutral adviser?

- Should the clause itself designate (and define) a specific ADR process such as mediation, conciliation, mini-trial or expert opinion, or leave the exact nature of the process for subsequent agreement?

- Should the clause set out detailed procedural rules (for example, as to the exchange of submissions, provision of documents, attendance at meetings, etc.), adopt those of an outside agency, or leave procedural matters for subsequent agreement by the parties or determination by the neutral adviser?

- Should there be joint or separate meetings between the parties and the neutral adviser?

- Is the neutral adviser to be allowed or required to make recommendations or evaluations of the parties' respective cases and the likely outcome of any subsequent litigation or arbitration?

- Should the clause contain express confidentiality provisions and/or specifically reserve the parties' strict legal rights in case the ADR procedure breaks down?

- Depending upon the nature of the dispute, should there be express provision for substantive obligations to be performed during the ADR procedure (for example, so as to require the contractor under a construction project to continue working pending resolution of the dispute)?

- Should there be an express provision restricting the use of information in any later court or arbitration proceedings (e.g. restricting its use to the enforcement of any resulting settlement agreement?)

- Should there be an express provision limiting the role of the neutral adviser in any later court or arbitration proceedings?

- Should the clause deal expressly with the authority of the parties' representatives to negotiate, make admissions, etc.?

- What is the timetable for procedural steps?

- Should the clause exclude particular types of disputes and/or remedies from the ADR procedure (i.e. so as to allow immediate recourse to litigation or arbitration in certain cases)?

- The clause *must* include a litigation or arbitration clause with an identifiable 'trigger' (for example, by providing when the ADR procedure is deemed to end).

- How are costs and fees to be dealt with?

None of the 'institutional' clauses reproduced in Appendix 3 is, in our view, ideal, although some are better than others for common types of disputes. We provide two alternative general purpose ADR clauses (a short form and a more detailed version) in Appendix 4. Ultimately, however, neither institutional nor general purpose clauses should be used without thoughtful review and tailoring to specific circumstances.

Pitfalls

- Do not forget that starting an ADR process will not (without specific agreement) stop time running for limitation purposes.

- Do not forget that, under many systems of law (including English law), mere agreements to negotiate are not enforceable; it is necessary to incorporate some specific provision, such as a duty to appoint a mediator within a certain period, to give an ADR provision any bite whatsoever.

- Do not forget that the result will not be enforceable unless and until the parties sign a formal settlement agreement.

- Do not forget that the use of ADR raises various issues concerning evidence; recommendations by a neutral third party are often based on mere assertions and informal statements by the parties, with no opportunity for cross-examination. Furthermore, if the ADR process is unsuccessful, complications may arise at a later stage in relation to material produced to the neutral third party informally, or admissions, during the course of the process.

- Do not forget that ADR does not suit all contractual relationships, and that generic ADR clauses do not necessarily suit any one specific relationship.

- Most importantly, do not forget to include a binding arbitration clause or reference to some other binding dispute resolution procedure to take effect if the ADR mechanism fails.

Appendix

1

Model arbitration clauses

A general purpose institutional clause is proposed in Chapter
7: Drafting the Arbitration Clause. The international contract
negotiator should also be aware of the following model clauses
recommended by some of the institutions and organisations
referred to in this Guide.

American Arbitration Association

**"Any controversy or claim arising out of or relating to
this contract shall be determined by arbitration in accordance with the International Arbitration Rules of
the American Arbitration Association."**
The parties may wish to consider adding:
"(a) The number of arbitrators shall be ... (one or three);
(b) The place of arbitration shall be ... (city and/or country);
(c) The language of the arbitration shall be...".

CIETAC

**"Any dispute, controversy or claim arising out of or in
connection with this Contract, including any question
regarding its existence, validity or termination, shall
be submitted to China International Economic and
Trade Arbitration Commission for arbitration which
shall be conducted in accordance with the Commission's arbitration rules in effect at the time of applying**

for arbitration. The arbitral award is final and binding upon both parties."

Consider adding the words "controversy or claim" after dispute. The parties should decide whether the place of arbitration is Beijing or at one of the regional sub-commissions in Shanghai or Shenzhen (this limited choice is permitted by Article 12 of the Rules). The language of the arbitration may also be chosen but in the absence of a choice, Chinese will be used. The Secretariat of the Arbitration Commission may require translations into Chinese of documents relied on by the parties to be supplied to it. The number of arbitrators should also be chosen. A suitable clause could read as follows:

"The tribunal shall consist of three arbitrators. Two arbitrators shall be selected by the respective parties. [The presiding arbitrator shall be selected by agreement between the parties or, failing agreement within [10] days of the appointment of the two party-nominated arbitrators, by the chairman of CIETAC]." OR

"The tribunal shall consist of one arbitrator who shall be selected by agreement between the parties."

Hong Kong International Arbitration Centre

(a) Any dispute, controversy or claim arising out of or relating to this contract, or the breach, termination or invalidity thereof, shall be settled by arbitration in accordance with the UNCITRAL Arbitration Rules as at present in force and as may be amended by the rest of this clause.

(b) The appointing authority shall be the Hong Kong International Arbitration Centre (HKIAC).

(c) The place of arbitration shall be in Hong Kong at the HKIAC.

(d) There shall be only one arbitrator. (1)

(e) Any such arbitration shall be administered by the HKIAC in accordance with the HKIAC Procedures for Arbitration in force at the date of this contract including such additions to the UNCITRAL Arbitration Rules as are therein contained. (2)

(f) The language(s) to be used in the arbitral proceedings shall be ... ...

(1) This sentence must be amended if a panel of three tribunal is required.
(2) This sentence may be deleted if administration by the HKIAC is not required.

Paragraph (e) relates solely to the administrative function of the HKIAC itself, and not to the way in which arbitrators conduct proceedings. If this paragraph (e) is left out, an *ad hoc* arbitration would be created, with the HKIAC acting solely as appointing authority. However, the importance of the appointing authority function, and of the ability to make facilities available, should not be underestimated.

We recommend that the applicable substantive law should also be stated expressly, and that the same consideration be given to varying the UNCITRAL majority decision rule, as suggested in the text following the UNCITRAL model clause below.

International Arbitral Centre of the Austrian Federal Economic Chamber

"All disputes arising out of this contract or related to its violation, termination or nullity shall be finally settled under the Rules of Arbitration and Conciliation of the International Arbitral Centre of the Austrian Federal Economic Chamber in Vienna (Vienna Rules) by one or more arbitrators appointed in accordance with these rules."

Appropriate supplementary provisions:
(a) the number or arbitrators shall be .... (one or three);
(b) the substantive law of .... shall be applicable;
(c) the language to be used in the arbitral proceedings shall be ...."

Parties having concluded the arbitration agreement as businessmen may waive their right to have recourse against an award in Austria on those grounds which recourse may be had against a court judgement by way of an application for reopening the case. If this is desired, it is recommended that the following be added:

"Pursuant to para. 598 (2) of the Austrian Code of Civil Procedure (ZPO), the parties expressly waive the application of para. 595 (1) figure 7 of the said Code."

This clause tracks exactly the ICC Standard Clause. It should therefore be complemented and amended in the same way as the ICC clause (see above), with the special observation that the rules of this Centre would not normally be adopted unless the parties intend that the arbitration will take place in Vienna.

ICC

"All disputes arising out of or in connection with the present contract shall be finally settled under the Rules of Arbitration of the International Chamber of Commerce by one or more arbitrators appointed in accordance with the said Rules."

'Parties are reminded that it may be desirable for them to stipulate in the arbitration clause itself the law governing the contract, the number of arbitrators and the place and language of the arbitration. The parties' free choice of the law governing the contract and of the place and language of the arbitration is not limited by the ICC Rules of Arbitration.

Attention is called to the fact that the laws of certain countries require that parties to contracts expressly accept arbitration clauses, sometimes in a precise and particular manner.'

To ensure the that the clause is as widely drawn as possible, the words "controversies or claims" (used in the UNCITRAL model clause) may be added after "disputes", so as to neutralise any argument as to arbitral jurisdiction, for example over undisputed claims.

We recommend that whenever the ICC model clause is used, it should be amended so that the words "one or more arbitrators" should, if possible, be reduced to a positive choice, of "a sole arbitrator" or "three arbitrators".

ICSID

"The parties hereto consent to submit to the International Centre for Settlement of Investment Disputes any dispute relating to or arising out of this Agreement for settlement by arbitration pursuant to the Convention on the Settlement of Investment Disputes between States and Nationals of Other States."

The ICSID mechanism is complex. ICSID has issued a special publication (Doc. ICSID /5/Rev.1) containing a number of highly refined additional model clauses adapted to different circumstances (consent in anticipation of subsequent ratification by a state which has not ratified the ICSID Convention; special clauses relating to the nature of the dispute; special clauses relating to contracts signed by government agencies or subdivisions; deemed nationality of the investor; preservation of the rights of the investor after compensation; exhaustion of local remedies; and so forth).

It is no coincidence that many ICSID arbitrations have immediately run into jurisdictional objections which could have been avoided by appropriate drafting. We therefore recommend that no ICSID arbitration clause should be agreed without taking specialist advice.

Inter-American Commercial Arbitration Commission

"Any dispute, controversy or claim arising out of or relating to this contract, or the breach, termination or Invalidity thereof, shall be settled by arbitration in accordance with the Rules of Procedure of the Inter-American Commercial Arbitration Commission in effect on the date of this Agreement."
Note: Parties may wish to consider adding:
"(a) the number of arbitrators shall be ... (one or three);
(b) the place of arbitration shall be ... (town or country);
(c) the language(s) to be used in the arbitral proceedings shall be ...."

Given the particular structure of IACAC, it appears to be especially important to stipulate the place of arbitration. We also suggest, as a general rule:
– specifying the applicable substantive law;
– considering a variation of the requirement of a majority award *(see* the text under the UNCITRAL model clause *below).*

LCIA

"Any dispute arising out of or in connection with this contract, including any question regarding its existence, validity or termination, shall be referred to and finally resolved by arbitration under the LCIA Rules, which Rules are deemed to be incorporated by reference into this clause.
The number of arbitrators shall be (one/three).
The place of arbitration shall be (city and/or country).

The language to be used in the arbitral proceedings shall be [ ].

The governing law of the contract [is/shall be] the substantive law of [ ]."

As with the ICC's standard clause, the words "controversy, or claim" may be added after "dispute".

Netherlands Arbitration Institute

"All disputes arising in connection with the present contract, or further contracts resulting therefrom, shall be finally settled in accordance with the Rules of the Netherlands Arbitration Institute (Nederlands Arbitrage Instituut)."

Additionally, various matters may be provided for:

– "The arbitral tribunal shall be composed of one arbitrator/three arbitrators."
– "The place of arbitration shall be....(city)."
– "The arbitral procedure shall be conducted in the [ ] language"
– "Consolidation of the arbitral proceedings with other arbitral proceedings pending in the Netherlands, as provided in art. 1046 of the Netherlands Code of Civil Procedure, is excluded." (1)

(1) The Netherlands is one of a handful of jurisdictions which permits court ordered consolidation of arbitrations. In general, it would be wise to exclude the right of the Dutch court to consolidate international arbitrations since the enforceability of the award may well depend upon the consensual nature of the arbitral process.

Singapore International Arbitration Centre

"Any dispute arising out of or in connection with this contract, including any question regarding its existence, validity or termination, shall be referred to and finally resolved by arbitration in [Singapore] in accordance with the Arbitration Rules of Singapore International Arbitration Centre ("SIAC Rules") for the time being in force which rules are deemed to be incorporated by reference to this clause."

 Parties may add:

"The Tribunal shall consist of .... arbitrator(s) to be appointed by the Chairman of SIAC.

The governing law of this contract shall be the substantive law of ....

The language of the arbitration shall be ...."

Stockholm Chamber of Commerce

"Any dispute, controversy or claim arising out of or in connection with this contract, or the breach, termination or invalidity thereof, shall be finally settled by arbitration in accordance with the Rules of the Arbitration Institute of the Stockholm Chamber of Commerce."

 The parties are advised to make the following additions to the clause, as required:

"The arbitral tribunal shall be composed of .... arbitrators (a sole arbitrator).

The place of arbitration shall be ....

The language(s) to be used in the arbitral proceedings shall be ...."

It would be rare for an arbitration under these Rules to take place outside Sweden; indeed the reason for choosing the Stockholm Institute has generally been thought to be the geo-political situation of Sweden in the arbitration context. As with other model clauses, we recommend a provision identifying the applicable substantive law.

Stockholm Chamber of Commerce (Expedited Rules)

"Any dispute, controversy or claim arising out of or in connection with this contract, or the breach, termination or invalidity thereof, shall be finally settled by arbitration in accordance with the Rules for Expedited Arbitrations of the Arbitration Institute of the Stockholm Chamber of Commerce."
"The place of arbitration shall be ....
The language(s) to be used in the arbitral proceedings shall be
......."

The Stockholm Chamber of Commerce is one of the few arbitral institutions to provide specific rules for fast track arbitration. These were introduced in 1995 and aim to ensure a rapid resolution of the dispute. There is a sole arbitrator appointed by the Stockholm Chamber of Commerce alone and time limits are considerably shortened.

UNCITRAL

"Any dispute, controversy or claim arising out of or relating to this contract, or the breach termination or invalidity thereof, shall be settled by arbitration in accordance with the UNCITRAL Arbitration Rules as at present in force."
Parties may wish to consider adding:
"(a) The appointing authority shall be ... (name of Institution or person);
(b) The number of arbitrators shall be ... (one or three);
(c) The place of arbitration shall be (town or country);
(d) The language(s) to be used in the arbitral proceedings shall be ...".

If the parties wish the appointing authority to be the ICC, the appropriate wording (which is recommended by the ICC to deal with the special features of the ICC's internal structure) should, instead of sub-clause (a) above, be as follows:

"The appointing authority shall be the ICC acting in accordance with the rules adopted by the ICC for this purpose."

Consideration may be given to varying the UNCITRAL Rules (which absolutely require majority awards) by providing as follows:

"When three arbitrators have been appointed, the award is given by a majority decision. If there be no majority, the award shall be made by the Chairman of the arbitral tribunal alone."

It should be noted that parties who like the UNCITRAL Arbitration Rules but are uncomfortable with the notion of *ad hoc* arbitration may refer to an institution as an administering rather than merely as an appointing authority. The ICC does not act in such a role, but other institutions will do so. The LCIA has made it clear that it is willing to administer arbitrations under the UNCITRAL Rules, and has published explanations of how it acts in such circumstances. The LCIA suggests that for those purposes the following be included in addition to clause (a) above:

"Any such arbitration shall be administered by the LCIA in accordance with the UNCITRAL Arbitration Rules in force at the date of this contract. Unless the arbitral tribunal directs otherwise all communications between the parties and the arbitral tribunal (except at hearings and meetings) shall be made through the LCIA. Any such communications shall be deemed received by the addressee when received by the LCIA. When passed on by the LCIA to any party such notices or communications will be sent to the address of that party specified in the Notice of Arbitration or such other address as may have been notified in writing by that party to the LCIA."

Given the absence of any express language in the UNCITRAL Rules, it is advisable to add a specific waiver of rights to appeal, etc. along the following lines (modelled on the equivalent LCIA provision):

"By agreeing to arbitration pursuant to this clause, the parties waive irrevocably their right to any form of appeal, review or recourse to any state court or other judicial authority, insofar as such waiver may be validly made."

WIPO Arbitration and Mediation Center

"Any dispute, controversy or claim arising under, out of or relating to this contract and any subsequent amendments of this contract, including, without limitation, its formation, validity, binding effect, interpretation, performance, breach or termination, as well as non-contractual claims, shall be referred to and finally determined by arbitration in accordance with the WIPO Arbitration Rules. The arbitral tribunal shall consist of [three arbitrators] [a sole arbitrator]. The place of arbitration shall be ... The language to be used in the arbitral proceedings shall be ... The dispute, controversy or claim shall be decided in accordance with the law of ..."

WIPO has also published a set of Expedited Arbitration Rules which may be adopted in cases of urgency.

2

Model clause for *ad hoc* arbitration

1. Any dispute, difference, controversy or claim arising out
of or in connection with this agreement shall be referred to
and determined by arbitration in ... [place].

2. The arbitral tribunal (hereinafter referred to as 'the tribunal') shall be composed of three arbitrators appointed as follows:
(i)   each party shall appoint an arbitrator, and the two arbitrators so appointed shall appoint a third arbitrator who
shall act as president of the tribunal;
(ii) if either party fails to appoint an arbitrator within 30
days of receiving notice of the appointment of an arbitrator by the other party, such arbitrator shall at the request
of that party be appointed by ... [the appointing author-
ity];
(iii) if the two arbitrators to be appointed by the parties fail to
agree upon a third arbitrator within 30 days of the appointment of the second arbitrator, the third arbitrator
shall be appointed by the ... [appointing authority] at the
written request of either party;
(iv) should a vacancy arise because any arbitrator dies, resigns,
refuses to act, or becomes incapable of performing his func-
tions, the vacancy shall be filled by the method by which
that arbitrator was originally appointed. When a vacancy is
filled the newly established tribunal shall exercise its discretion to determine whether any hearings shall be re-
peated.

3. As soon as practicable after the appointment of the arbitrator to be appointed by him, and in any event no later than 30 days after the tribunal has been constituted, the claimant shall deliver to the respondent (with copies to each arbitrator) a statement of case, containing particulars of his claims and written submissions in support thereof, together with any documents relied on.

4. Within 30 days of the receipt of the claimant's statement of case, the respondent shall deliver to the claimant (with copies to each arbitrator) a statement of case in answer, together with any counterclaim and any documents relied upon.

5. Within 30 days of the receipt by the claimant of any statement of counterclaim by the respondent, the claimant may deliver to the respondent (with copies to each arbitrator) a reply to counterclaim together with any additional documents relied upon.

6. As soon as practicable after its constitution, the tribunal shall convene a meeting with the parties or their representatives to determine the procedure to be followed in the arbitration.

7. The procedure shall be as agreed by the parties or, in default of agreement, as determined by the tribunal. However, the following procedural matters shall in any event be taken as agreed:
(i) the language of the arbitration shall be ... [language];
(ii) the tribunal may in its discretion hold a hearing and make an award in relation to any preliminary issue at the request of either party and shall do so at the joint request of both parties;
(iii) the tribunal shall hold a hearing, or hearings, relating to substantive issues unless the parties agree otherwise in writing;
(iv) the tribunal shall issue its final award within 60 days of the last hearing of the substantive issues in dispute between the parties.

8.   In the event of default by either party in respect of any procedural order made by the tribunal, the tribunal shall have power to proceed with the arbitration and to make its award.

9.   If an arbitrator appointed by one of the parties fails or refuses to participate in the arbitration at any time after the hearings on to participate in the substance of the dispute have started, the remaining two arbitrators may continue the arbitration and make an award without a vacancy being deemed to arise if, in their discretion, they determine that the failure or refusal of the other arbitrator to participate is without reasonable excuse.

10. Any award or procedural decision of the tribunal shall if necessary be made by a majority and, in the event that no majority may be formed, the presiding arbitrator shall proceed as if he were a sole arbitrator.

3

Model clauses for conciliation or mediation

American Arbitration Association

"If a dispute arises out of or relates to this contract, or the breach thereof, and if the said dispute cannot be settled through negotiation, the parties agree first to try in good faith to settle the dispute by mediation under the Commercial Mediation Rules of the American Arbitration Association, before resorting to arbitration, litigation, or some other dispute resolution procedure."

Centre For Dispute Resolution

"1. If any dispute arises out of this agreement the parties will attempt to settle it by negotiation.

[A party may not serve an ADR notice or commence Court proceedings/an arbitration until [21] days after it has made a written offer to the other party[ies] to negotiate a settlement to the dispute.]

2. If the parties are unable to settle any dispute by negotiation [within [21] days], the parties will attempt to settle it by mediation in accordance with the Centre for Dispute Resolution (CEDR) Model Mediation Procedure.

3. To initiate a mediation a party [by its Managing Director/...] must give notice in writing (ADR notice) to the other party[ies] to the dispute [addressed to its/their respective Managing Director/...] requesting a mediation in accordance with Clause 2".

In its Guidance Note on its Model ADR Contract Clauses, CEDR proposes certain optional/additional wording. Most importantly, the mediation clause should specify that if the parties have not settled the dispute within a given period of time from commencement of the mediation, the dispute shall be referred to arbitration or some other binding procedure.

CPR Institute for Dispute Resolution

Mediation – Arbitration or Litigation
The parties will attempt in good faith to resolve any controversy or claim arising out of or relating to this agreement by mediation in accordance with the CPR Mediation Procedure.

If the dispute has not been resolved pursuant to the aforesaid mediation procedure within 60 days of the commencement of such procedure (which period may be extended by mutual agreement), or if either party will not participate in a mediation,

[Select one of the following alternatives.]

(i) the controversy shall be settled by arbitration in accordance with the CPR Institute for Dispute Resolution Rules for Non-Administered Arbitration, by [a sole arbitrator] [three arbitrators, of whom each party shall appoint one] [three arbitrators, none of whom shall be appointed by either party]. [Any mediator or arbitrator not appointed by a party shall be selected from the CPR Panels of Distinguished Neutrals]. The arbitration shall be governed by the United States Arbitration Act, 9 U.S.C. §§ 1–16 to the exclusion of state laws inconsistent there-

with, and judgement upon the award rendered by the arbitrator[s] may be entered by any court having jurisdiction thereof. The place of arbitration shall be _____ _____ .
The arbitrator[s] [are] [are not] empowered to award damages in excess of compensatory damages.

(ii) either party may initiate litigation [upon [___] days' written notice to the other party]."

CPR also publishes variations of this dispute resolution clause involving face-to-face negotiation prior to mediation.

City Disputes Panel

(a) Non-binding reference to conciliation/mediation

"The parties will consider using [conciliation in accordance with the CDP procedures then in force] [mediation in accordance with the CDP Mediation Rules] for any dispute or difference arising out of or in connection with this contract. If [either/any] party does not wish to use, or continue to use, [conciliation/mediation], or [conciliation/mediation] does not resolve the dispute, the parties shall refer any such dispute or difference to arbitration under [specify arbitration rules]."

Again, the parties should specify a time period within which an attempt to settle the dispute by conciliation or mediation may be made, so that an arbitration or other binding procedure can be commenced immediately thereafter.

The CDP Mediation Rules are reproduced on pages [ ] below.

(b) Binding reference to conciliation/mediation

"Any dispute or difference arising out of or in connection with this contract shall be referred to [conciliation in accordance with The City Disputes Panel Limited (CDP) procedures then in force] [mediation in accordance with the CDP Mediation Rules] before resorting to arbitration.

The [conciliation/mediation] process will be commenced by service by one party on the other(s) of a written notice that the dispute is to be referred to [conciliation/mediation] (the "Commencement Notice"). The parties will then participate in good faith in the [conciliation/mediation]. The [conciliator/mediator] shall be a member of CDP. In the event that the parties are unable to agree a choice of [conciliator/mediator] within [ ] days of the date of service of the Commencement Notice, the parties shall accept a conciliator/mediator nominated by CDP.

If, and only if, the dispute is not resolved within [ ] days of the date of service of the Commencement Notice (or such longer period as the parties may agree) the parties shall refer the dispute to arbitration under [specify arbitration rules]."

Although this clause has been drafted with a view to creating binding obligations, the CDP's guidance notes acknowledge that it is uncertain under English law whether clauses which require parties to use conciliation before resorting to litigation are specifically enforceable.

Optional protective provisions:

"(a) Nothing in clauses [ ] shall prevent [either/any] party from having recourse to a court of competent jurisdiction for the sole purpose of seeking a preliminary injunction or such other provisional judicial relief as it considers necessary to avoid irreparable damage.

(b) In calculating the limitation period for any claim that is ultimately referred to arbitration, the period between the date of service of the Commencement Notice and the date on which the parties are free to refer the claim to arbitration shall be excluded."

ICSID Model Clause for Conciliation

"The parties hereto hereby consent to submit to the International Centre for Settlement of Investment Disputes any dispute in relation to or arising out of this Agreement for settlement by conciliation pursuant to the Convention on the Settlement of Investment Disputes between States and Nationals of Other States.

The basic clause set forth above assumes that:
(i) the governmental party to the dispute is the contracting state itself (rather than a constituent subdivision or an agency);
(ii) the investor is clearly a national of another contracting state;
(iii) the parties accept the residual choice-of-law rule set forth in Article 42 of the Convention; and
(iv) they do not wish to derogate from the ICSID Conciliation/ Arbitration Rules."

UNCITRAL Conciliation Rules

"Where, in the event of a dispute arising out of or relating to this contract, the parties wish to seek an amicable settlement of that dispute by conciliation, the conciliation shall take place in accordance with the UNCITRAL Conciliation Rules as at present in force."

4

General purpose ADR clauses

Short form

If any dispute or difference arises out of or in connection with this agreement the parties shall [with the assistance of the Centre for Dispute Resolution] seek to resolve the dispute or difference amicably by using an alternative dispute resolution (ADR) procedure acceptable to both parties [before pursuing any other remedies available to them].

If either party fails or refuses to agree to or participate in the ADR procedure or if in any event the dispute or difference is not resolved to the satisfaction of both parties within [90] days after it has arisen the dispute or difference shall be referred to arbitration ... [add arbitration clause].

Long form

If any dispute or difference arises out of or in connection with this agreement [which the parties are unable to resolve by negotiation][1] (the "dispute"), the parties shall seek to resolve

---

[1] Alternatively, the clause may expressly provide that for a specified period the parties shall attempt in good faith to resolve the dispute by negotiation (for example, by suitably authorised representatives of the parties attending a joint meeting to discuss the dispute).

the dispute amicably by using the following procedure [before pursuing any other remedies available to them]:-
1. The parties shall submit the dispute to a neutral adviser appointed by agreement between the parties to assist them in resolving the dispute. Either party may give written notice to the other describing the nature of the dispute, requiring the dispute to be submitted to such a neutral adviser and proposing the names of up to three suitable persons to be appointed.[2] If no such person is appointed by agreement between the parties within [14] days after such notice is given (or, if no such notice is given, within 28 days after the dispute has arisen), either party may request [the Centre for Dispute Resolution] to appoint a neutral adviser.
2. The parties shall, with the assistance of the neutral adviser appointed in accordance with paragraph 1 above, seek in good faith to resolve the dispute by using an alternative dispute resolution (ADR) procedure agreed between the parties or, in default of such agreement, established by the neutral adviser.[3]
3. If the parties accept any recommendations made by the neutral adviser or otherwise reach agreement as to the resolution of the dispute, such agreement shall be recorded in writing and signed by the parties (and, if applicable, the neutral adviser), whereupon it shall become binding upon the parties.

---

[2] Various bodies (e.g. CEDR, ADR Net and The Academy of Experts) maintain lists of qualified persons and can provide assistance in appointing the neutral adviser.

[3] Alternatively, the clause itself can deal with procedural matters such as the exchange of submissions, provision of documents, attendance at meetings, etc. It may also be appropriate to add a confidentiality provision and/or provide expressly that the neutral adviser may make (non-binding) recommendations, or, at the joint request of the parties, binding recommendations as to the resolution of the dispute.

4. If:-
    (a) the dispute has not been resolved to the satisfaction of both parties within [60] days after the appointment of the neutral adviser; or
    (b) either party fails or refuses to agree to or participate in the ADR procedure; or
    (c) in any event the dispute is not resolved within [90] days after it has arisen,

    then the dispute shall be referred to arbitration ... [add arbitration clause].

5. In the event that the dispute is referred to arbitration [in accordance with paragraph *4 above*]:
    (a) any neutral adviser involved in the ADR procedure shall not, unless the parties jointly agree otherwise, take any part in the arbitration or any other related proceedings, whether as an arbitrator, witness or otherwise, and no aspect of the ADR procedure, including any recommendations made by him in connection with the ADR procedure, shall be relied upon by either party without the consent of the other party and the neutral adviser;
    (b) neither party shall make use of nor rely upon information supplied, or arguments raised, by the other party in the ADR procedure.

6. The costs and fees of the neutral adviser, the ADR service provider and any neutral venue shall be borne equally by the parties. The parties shall bear their own costs of all other aspects of the ADR procedure.

5

Signatories to the New York Convention (as at April 1999)

Convention on the Recognition and Enforcement of Foreign Arbitral Awards (New York, 1958)

State	Notes	Signature	Ratification / Accession
Algeria	1/2		1989
American Samoa	(a)1/2		1970
Antigua and Barbuda	1/2		1989
Argentina	1/2/7	1958	1989
Armenia	1/2		1997
Australia			1975
Australian Antarctic Territory	(b)		1975
Austria			1961
Bahrain	1/2		1988
Bangladesh			1992
Barbados	1/2		1993
Belarus	1/3	1958	1960
Belgium	1	1958	1975
Belize	(c)1		1981
Benin			1974
Bermuda	(d)1		1980
Bolivia			1995
Bosnia Herzegovina	1/2/6		1993
Botswana	1/2		1971

State	Notes	Signature	Ratification/ Accession
Brunei	1		1996
Bulgaria	1/3	1958	1961
Burkina Faso			1987
Cambodia			1960
Cameroon			1988
Canada	4		1986
Canton Island	(b)1/2		1970
Cayman Islands	1		1981
Central African Republic	1/2		1962
Chile			1975
China	1/2		1987
Christmas Island	(b)		1975
Cocos (Keeling) Island			1975
Colombia			1979
Comoros Islands	(e)		1959
Costa Rica		1958	1987
Cote d'Ivoire			1991
Croatia	1/2/6		1993
Cuba	1/2/3		1974
Cyprus	1/2		1980
Czech Republic	(f)1		1993
Denmark	1/2		1972
Djibouti			1983
Dominica			1988
Ecuador	1/2	1958	1962
Egypt			1959
Enderberry Island	(a)1/2		1970
El Salvador		1958	1998
Estonia			1993
Faeroe Islands	(g)1/2		1976
Finland		1958	1962
France	1	1958	1959
French Polynesia	(e)1		1959
Georgia			1994
Germany	(h)/1	1958	1961

SIGNATORIES TO THE NEW YORK CONVENTION

State	Notes	Signature	Ratification/ Accession
Ghana			1968
Gibraltar	(i)1		1975
Greece	1/2		1962
Greenland	(g)1/2		1976
Guam	(a)1/2		1970
Guatemala	1/2		1984
Guernsey	(j)1		1985
Guinea			1991
Haiti			1983
Holy See	1/2		1975
Hong Kong	(k)1		1977
Hungary	1/2		1962
India	1/2	1958	1960
Indonesia	1/2		1981
Ireland	1		1981
Isle of Man	(l)1		1979
Israel		1958	1959
Italy			1969
Japan	1		1961
Jordan		1958	1979
Kazakhstan			1995
Kenya	1		1989
Korea	1/2		1995
Kuwait	1		1978
Kyrgyzstan			1996
Latvia			1992
Lao People's Democratic Republic			1998
Lebanon			1998
Lesotho			1989
Lithuania	1/2		1995
Luxembourg	1	1958	1983
Macedonia (former Yugoslav Republic)	1/2/6		1994
Madagascar	1/2		1962

State	Notes	Signature	Ratification / Accession
Malagasy Republic			1962
Malaysia			1985
Mali	1		1994
Mauritania			1997
Mauritius	1/2		1996
Mexico			1971
Monaco	1/2	1958	1982
Mongolia	1/2		1994
Morocco	1		1959
Mozambique			1998
Nepal	1/2		1998
Netherlands	1	1958	1964
Netherlands Antilles	(m)1		1964
New Zealand	1		1983
Niger			1964
Nigeria	1/2		1970
Norfolk Island	(b)		1975
Norway	1/5		1961
Oman			1999
Pakistan			1958
Panama			1984
Paraguay			1997
Peru			1988
Philippines	1/2	1958	1967
Poland	1/2	1958	1961
Portugal	1		1994
Puerto Rico	(a)1/2		1970
Republic of Moldavia			1998
Romania	1/2/3		1961
Russian Federation	(n)1/3	1958	1960
San Marino			1979
Saudi Arabia	1		1994
Senegal			1994
Singapore	1		1986
Slovakia	(f)		1993

SIGNATORIES TO THE NEW YORK CONVENTION

State	Notes	Signature	Ratification/ Accession
Slovenia			1992
South Africa			1976
Spain			1977
Sri Lanka		1958	1962
St Pierre et Miquelon	(e)		1959
Surinam	(o)1		1964
Sweden		1958	1972
Switzerland	1	1958	1965
Syrian Arab Republic			1959
Thailand			1959
Trinidad and Tobago	1/2		1966
Tunisia	1/2		1967
Turkey	1/2		1992
Uganda	1		1992
Ukraine	1/3	1958	1960
United Kingdom	1		1975
United Republic of Tanzania	1		1964
United States of America	1/2		1970
Uruguay			1983
Uzbekistan			1996
Venezuela	1/2		1995
Vietnam	1/2/3/9		1995
Virgin Islands	(a)1/2		1970
Wake Island	(a)1/2		1970
Wallis & Futuna Islands	(e)1		1959
Yugoslavia	1/2/6		1982
Zimbabwe			1994

Notes – see pp. 158–160

APPENDIX 5

Notes

Accessions

(a) Extension made by the United States of America upon acceding to the Convention.
(b) Extension made by Australia upon acceding to the Convention.
(c) Extension made by the United Kingdom on 24.02.1981.
(d) Extension made by the United Kingdom on 12.02.1980.
(e) Extension made by France on 26.06.1959.
(f) The Convention was signed by the former Czechoslovakia on 3 October 1958 and an instrument of notification was deposited on 10 July 1959. On 28 May 1993 Slovakia and on 30 September 1993, the Czech Republic deposited instruments of succession.
(g) Extension made by Denmark on 10.02.1976.
(h) The Convention was acceded to by the former German Democratic Republic on 20 February 1975 with reservations 1, 2 and 3.
(i) Extension made by the United Kingdom on 24.09.1975.
(j) Extension made by the United Kingdom on 19.04.1985.
(k) Extension made by the United Kingdom on 21.04.1977.
(l) Extension made by the United Kingdom on 23.05.1979.
(m) Extension made by the Netherlands on 24.04.1964.
(n) The Russian Federation continues, as from 24 December 1991, the membership of the former Union of Soviet Socialist Republics in the United Nations and maintains, as from that date, full responsibility for all the rights and obligations of the USSR under the Charter of the United Nations and multilateral treaties deposited with the Secretary General.
(o) On 25.01.1975, Surinam became independent. By letter of 29.01.1975, from the then Prime Minister to the Secretary General of the UN, Surinam has declared that it will

remain bound to the Treaties and Conventions which the Netherlands has made applicable.

Declarations and reservations

(Excluding territorial declarations and certain other reservations and declarations of a political nature)

1. State will apply the Convention to recognition and enforcement of awards made in the territory of another contracting state.
2. State will apply the Convention only to differences arising out of legal relationships whether contractual or not which are considered as commercial under the national law.
3. With regard to awards made in the territory of non-contracting states, state will apply the Convention only to the extent to which these states grant reciprocal treatment.
4. The Government of Canada has declared that Canada will apply the Convention only to differences arising out of legal relationships, whether contractual or not, which are considered as commercial under the laws of Canada, except in the case of the Province of Quebec where the law does not provide for such limitation.
5. State will not apply the Convention to differences where the subject matter of the proceedings is immovable property situated in the state, or a right in or to such property.
6. State will apply the Convention only to those arbitral awards which were adopted after the Convention came into effect.
7. Argentina declared that the Convention should be construed in accordance with the principles and rules of the national constitution in force or with those resulting from reforms mandated by the constitution.

8. On 23 April 1993, Switzerland notified the Secretary-General if its decision to withdraw the declaration it had made upon ratification.
9. Vietnam declared that interpretation of the Convention before the Vietnamese courts or competent authorities should be made in accordance with the constitution and the law of Vietnam.

6

Countries having adopted the UNCITRAL model
law (as at April 1999)

**UNCITRAL Model Law on International Commercial
Arbitration (1985)**

Australia
Bahrain
Bermuda
Bulgaria
Canada (all provinces and territories)
Cyprus
Egypt
Germany
Guatemala
Hong Kong
Hungary
India
Iran
Ireland
Kenya
Lithuania
Malta
Mexico
New Zealand
Nigeria
Oman

Peru
Russian Federation
Scotland
Singapore
Sri Lanka
Tunisia
Ukraine
USA (California, Connecticut, Oregon and Texas)
Zimbabwe

Source: UNCITRAL

7

UNCITRAL notes on organising arbitral proceedings

List of matters for possible consideration in organising arbitral proceedings

This list is part of the *UNCITRAL Notes on Organising Arbitral Proceedings,* which the United Nations Commission on International Trade Law (*UNCITRAL*) adopted in 1996. The *Notes,* published as United Nations documents V.96–84935, contain introductory explanations and annotations to the items that appear in this list. The list is reproduced separately to facilitate its use by those practitioners who wish to use the list without having at hand the full text of the *Notes.*

1. Set of arbitration rules

If the parties have not agreed on a set of arbitration rules, would they wish to do so.

2. Language of proceedings

(a) Possible need for translation of documents, in full or in part
(b) Possible need for interpretation of oral presentations

(c) Cost of translation and interpretation

3. Place of arbitration

(a) Determination of the place of arbitration, if not already agreed upon by the parties
(b) Possibility of meetings outside the place of arbitration

4. Administrative services that may be needed for the arbitral tribunal to carry out its functions

5. Deposits in respect of costs

(a) Amount to be deposited
(b) Management of deposits
(c) Supplementary deposits

6. Confidentiality of information relating to the arbitration; possible agreement thereon

7. Routing of written communications among the parties and the arbitrators

8. Telefax and other electronic means of sending documents

(a) Telex
(b) Other electronic means (e.g. electronic mail and magnetic or optical disk)

9. Arrangements for the exchange of written submissions

(a) Scheduling of written submissions
(b) Consecutive or simultaneous submissions

10. Practical details concerning written submissions and evidence (e.g. method of submission, copies, numbering, references)

11. Defining points at issue; order of deciding issues; defining relief or remedy sought

(a) Should a list of point s at issue be prepared
(b) In which order should the points at issue be decided
(c) Is there a need to define more precisely the relief or remedy sought

12. Possible settlement negotiations and their effect on scheduling proceedings

13. Documentary evidence

(a) Time-limits for submission of documentary evidence intended to be submitted by the parties; consequences of late submission
(b) Whether the arbitral tribunal intends to require a party to produce documentary evidence
(c) Should assertion about the origin and receipt of documents and about the correctness of photocopies be assumed as accurate

(d) Are the parties willing to submit jointly a single set of documentary evidence
(e) Should voluminous and complicated documentary evidence be presented through summaries, tabulations, charts, extracts or samples

14. Physical evidence other than documents

(a) What arrangements should be made if physical evidence will be submitted
(b) What arrangements should be made if an on-site inspection is necessary

15. Witnesses

(a) Advance notice about a witness whom a party intends to present; written witnesses' statements
(b) Manner of taking oral evidence of witnesses
    (i) Order in which questions will be asked and the manner in which the hearing of witnesses will be conducted
    (ii) Whether oral testimony will be given under oath or affirmation and, if so, in what form an oath or affirmation should be made
    (iii) May witnesses be in the hearing room when they are not testifying
(c) The order in which the witnesses will be called
(d) Interviewing witnesses prior to their appearance at a hearing
(e) Hearing representatives of a party

16. Experts and expert witnesses

(a) Expert appointed by the arbitral tribunal
    (i) The expert's terms of reference

    (ii) The opportunity of the parties to comment on the expert's report, including by presenting expert testimony

(b) Expert opinion presented by a party (expert witness)

17. Hearings

(a) Decision whether to hold hearings
(b) Whether one period of hearings should be held or separate periods of hearings
(c) Setting dates for hearings
(d) Whether there should be a limit on the aggregate amount of time each party will have for oral arguments and questioning witnesses
(e) The order in which the parties will present their arguments and evidence
(f) Length of hearings
(g) Arrangements for a record of the hearings
(h) Whether and when the parties are permitted to submit notes summarising their oral arguments

18. Multi-party arbitration

19. Possible requirements concerning filing or delivering the award

Who should take steps to fulfil any requirement.

8

Addresses of arbitral institutions and other organisations referred to in the text

American Arbitration Association
335 Madison Avenue
New York
NY 10017–4605
USA
Tel: +1 212 716 5800
Fax: +1 212 716 5905
Web: http://www.adr.org
E-mail: aaaheadquarters@adr.com

The Academy of Experts
2 South Square
Grays Inn
London WC1R 5HP
ENGLAND
Tel: +44 171 637 0333
Fax: +44 171 637 1893
Web: http://www.academy-experts.org/
E-mail: admin@academy-experts.org

Centre for Dispute Resolution
Princes House
95 Gresham Street
London EC2V 7NA
ENGLAND
Tel: +44 171 600 0500
Fax: +44 171 600 0501
Web: http://www.cedr.co.uk
E-mail: mediate@cedr.co.uk

City Disputes Panel
Fifth Floor
3 London Wall Buildings
London EC2M 5PD
ENGLAND
Tel: +44 171 638 4775
Fax: +44 171 638 4776
Web: http://members.aol.com/cdplondon/cdp.html
E-mail: FreemanCDP@aol.com

CPR Institute for Dispute Resolution
366 Madison Avenue
New York
NY 10017–3122
USA
Tel: +1 212 949 6490
Fax: +1 212 949 8859
Web: http://www.cpradr.org
E-mail: info@cpradr.org

ADDRESSES

Chartered Institute of Arbitrators
International Arbitration Centre
24 Angel Gate
City Road
London EC1V 2RS
ENGLAND
Tel: +44 171 837 4483
Fax: +44 171 837 4185
Web: http://www.arbitrators.org
E-mail: 71411.2735@compuserve.com

China International Economic and Trade Arbitration
Commission (CIETAC)
6/F., Golden Land Building
32, Liang Ma Qiao Road
Chaoyang District
Beijing 100016
CHINA
Tel: +86 10 6464 6688/+86 10 6464 3517
Fax: +86 10 6464 3500/+86 10 6464 3520
E-mail: cietac@public.bta.net.cn

Hong Kong International Arbitration Centre
38th Floor Two Exchange Square
8 Connaught Place
Hong Kong
CHINA
Tel: +852 2525 2381
Fax: +852 2524 2171
Web: http://www.hkiac.org
E-mail: adr@hkiac.org

International Arbitral Centre of the Austrian Federal
Economic Chamber
Wiedner Hauptstrasse 63
PO Box 319
A–1045 Vienna
AUSTRIA
Tel: +43 1 501 05 3701
Fax: +43 1 502 06 3702
E-mail: iccat@wk.or.at

Inter-American Commercial Arbitration Commission
OAS Administration Building, Room 211
19th and Constitution Avenue
Washington, DC 20006
USA
Tel: +1 202 458 3249
Fax: +1 202 458 3293

International Centre for Settlement of Investment Disputes
1818 H Street NW
Washington DC 20433
USA
Tel: +1 202 458 1534
Fax: +1 202 522 2615/2027

International Chamber of Commerce
International Court of Arbitration
38 Cours Albert 1er
75008 Paris
FRANCE
Tel: +33 1 49 53 28 28
Fax: +33 1 49 53 29 29
Web: http://www.iccwbo.org
E-mail: arb@iccwbo.org

ADDRESSES

International Commercial Arbitration Court at the Chamber
of Commerce and Industry of the Russian Federation
6 Ilynka Street
Moscow 103012
RUSSIAN FEDERATION
Tel: +7 095 929 0193
Fax: +7 095 929 0334

Jams Endispute
345 Park Avenue
8th Floor
New York
NY 10154
USA
Tel: +1 212 751 2700
Fax: +1 212 751 4099
Web: http://www.jams-endispute.com

Kuala Lumpur Regional Centre for Arbitration
12 Jalan Conlay
50450 Kuala Lumpur
MALAYSIA
Tel: +60 3 242 0103/242 0702
Fax: +60 3 242 4513
Web: http://www.klrca.org
E-mail: klrca@putra.net.my

London Court of International Arbitration
Hulton House, 6th Floor
161–166 Fleet Street
London EC4A 2DY
ENGLAND
Tel: +44 171 936 3530
Fax: +44 171 936 3533
Web: http://www.lcia-arbitration.com/lcia/
E-mail: lcia@lcia-arbitration.com

Netherlands Arbitration Institute
P.O. Box 190
3000 AD Rotterdam
Gebouw "Plaza"
Weena 666
3012 CN Rotterdam
The Netherlands
Tel: +31 10 404 2200
Fax: +31 10 404 5140

Permanent Court of Arbitration
Peace Palace
Carnegieplein 2
2517 KJ The Hague
THE NETHERLANDS
Tel: +31 70 346 9680
Fax: +31 70 356 1338

Singapore International Arbitration Centre
1 Coleman Street #05–08
The Adelphi
Singapore 179803
SINGAPORE
Tel: +65 334 1277
Fax: +65 334 2942
Web: http://siac.tdb.gov.sg
E-mail: sinarb@singnet.com.sg

Stockholm Chamber of Commerce (Arbitration Institute)
PO Box 16050
103 21 Stockholm
SWEDEN
Tel: +46 8 555 100 50
Fax: +46 8 566 316 50
Web: http://www.chamber.se
E-mail: arbitration@chamber.se

ADDRESSES

United Nations Commission on International Trade Law
Vienna International Centre
P O Box 500
A–1400 Vienna
AUSTRIA
Tel: +43 1 26060 4060
Fax: +43 1 26060 5813
Web: http://www.un.or.at/uncitral
E-mail: uncitral@unvienna.un.or.at

WIPO Arbitration and Mediation Center
World Intellectual Property Organisation
34 Chemin des Colombettes
1211 Geneva 20
SWITZERLAND
Tel: +41 22 338 8247
Fax: +41 22 740 3700
Web: http://www.arbiter.wipo.int
E-mail: arbiter.mail@wipo.int